Prayers of Comfort:

*Daily Petitions from the
Heidelberg Catechism*

Mrs. Nancy A. Almodovar, PhD

ISBN: 1508751250
ISBN-13: 978-1508751250

DEDICATION

First, I thank my husband, Rev. Roberto Almodovar, who always encourages me to keep writing. Who has guarded, supported and unconditionally loved me. I love you, always and forever.

Second, I am grateful to my Faithful Father, whom through the use of the Heidelberg Catechism and the Scriptures; I have come to know more and more as my Faithful and Heavenly Father who dwells in the Majesty on High. This year my husband and I decided to go through the Heidelberg Catechism during our evening family worship. It was this time, unlike the many other times we have gone through it that I began to see how each of the answers could be reworded to become prayers regarding those doctrines taught. This is the culmination of that time together at the dinner table in the evening, where I learned how to pray better and to enjoy praying.

Third, I want to dedicate this to my mom, who was recently diagnosed with lung cancer, and taught her daughter that we have a God and Father who answers the prayers of His children in often quite remarkable and unexpected ways. I love you, Mom.

Finally, to the many ladies who have come to our Facebook Group "Old Paths for Today's Women". Together, God has been reforming us according to His Word. We have learned so much over these past many years and God has used many of you to help me understand His works and Word better than I have before. Thank you for standing firm for the Faith once handed down to us and for being, as my Pastor, Jonanthan Van Hoogen taught me, "As the Man in the Arena": better to be in the arena fighting, even if not done well or with the most skill, than in the bleachers telling us what to do but not giving any real help. You ladies are precious in my sight but that does not compare with how much our Faithful Father loves you. I pray this will be a blessing to you as you seek Him.

"Comfort, comfort my people, says your God. Speak tenderly to Jerusalem, and cry to her that her warfare is ended, that her iniquity is pardoned, and that she has received from the LORD's Hand double for all her sins."
Isaiah 40:1-2 ESV

ACKNOWLEDGMENTS

University of Heidelberg. The Heidelberg Catechism

DAY 1: MY ONLY COMFORT

What is thy only comfort in life and death?

That I with body and soul, both in life and death, (a) am not my own, (b) but belong unto my faithful Saviour Jesus Christ; (c) who, with his precious blood, has fully satisfied for all my sins, (d) and delivered me from all the power of the devil; (e) and so preserves me (f) that without the will of my heavenly Father, not a hair can fall from my head; (g) yea, that all things must be subservient to my salvation, (h) and therefore, by his Holy Spirit, He also assures me of eternal life, (i) and makes me sincerely willing and ready, henceforth, to live unto him. (j)

(a) Rom. 14: 7,8. (b) 1 Cor. 6: 19. (c) 1 Cor. 3: 23; Tit. 2: 14. (d) 1 Pet. 1: 18,19; 1 John 1: 7; 1 John 2: 2,12. (e) Heb. 2: 14; 1 John 3: 8; John 8: 34-36. (f) John 6: 39; John 10: 28; 2 Thess. 3: 3; 1 Pet. 1: 5. (g) Matt. 10: 29-31; Luke 21: 18. (h) Rom. 8: 28. (i) 2 Cor. 1: 20-22; 2 Cor. 5: 5; Eph. 1: 13,14; Rom. 8: 16. (j) Rom. 8: 14; 1 John 3: 3.

Most Gracious and Eternal Father, None of us live to ourselves and no one dies to themselves for whether we live unto the Lord or whether we die, we die unto the Lord and therefore, we belong to you. Thank you, that He Who gave Himself for us, to redeem us from all iniquity, purifying us unto himself as a peculiar people have been made the temple of the Holy Ghost, which we have of God and are not our own. Because we know we have been redeemed apart from corruptible things, such as silver and gold, but by the precious blood of Christ, make us zealous unto good works so that as we walk in the light we have fellowship with one another and with Jesus Christ who cleanses us from all sins.

We praise you that you have destroyed the works of the devil and have delivered us from the one who had the power of death bringing us new life in Jesus Christ, and that life is eternal and no one can pluck us out of your hand for you are faithful who has established us and keeps us from evil. We know that because we belong to you, through Christ, by the power of the Holy Spirit, all things work together for good to those who love you and are called according to your purpose. You have sealed us by your Holy Spirit, established us with Christ and we are the sons of the Living God. May you teach us to purify ourselves, even as He is pure because of this hope and comfort you have given us, in Christ Jesus through the working of His Blessed Holy Spirit. Amen.

DAY 2: THE NECESSARY THINGS

Question 2: How many things are necessary for thee to know, that thou, enjoying this comfort, mayest live and die happily?

Answer: Three; (a) the first, how great my sins and miseries are; (b) the second, how I may be delivered from all my sins and miseries; (c) the third, how I shall express my gratitude to God for such deliverance. (d)

Question 3: Whence knowest thou thy misery?

Answer: Out of the law of God. (a)

(a) Rom. 3: 20.

Question 4: What does the law of God require of us?

Answer: Christ teaches us that briefly, Matthew 22:37-40, "Thou shalt love the Lord thy God with all thy heart, with all thy soul, and with all thy mind, and with all thy strength. This is the first and the great commandment; and the second is like unto it, Thou shalt love thy neighbour as thyself. On these two commandments hang all the law and the prophets." (a)

(a) Deut. 6: 5; Lev. 19: 18; Mark 12: 30; Luke 10: 27.

Question 5: Canst thou keep all these things perfectly?

Answer: In no wise; (a) for I am prone by nature to hate God and my neighbour.(b)

(a) Rom .3: 10,20,23; 1 John 1: 8,10. (b) Rom. 8: 7; Eph. 2: 3; Tit. 3: 3; Gen. 6: 5; Gen. 8: 21; Jer. 17: 9; Rom. 7: 23.

Faithful Father, Almighty God, you beckon us this day to "Come unto me, all ye that labour and are heavy laden" and promise to give us rest as we take Your yoke upon us, learning from You because Your yoke is easy and Your burden light. Grant us repentance and the remission of sins through the Name of Jesus Christ. Though we were sometimes foolish, disobedient, deceived, serving diver's lusts and pleasures, living in malice and envy, hateful and hating one another, it was through the kindness and love of You, our God and Savior, that we have received mercy by the washing of regeneration and renewing of the Holy Spirit. Grant us to be justified by faith through your grace and make us heirs according to the hope of eternal life. You opened our eyes to know our sin because of Your

Word, and we have no cloke for our sins but ask to be clothed upon with the Righteousness of Jesus Christ who covers our nakedness with His robes of righteousness for there is no salvation in any other Name under heaven and to Him, our Saviour Jesus Christ, do all the prophets witness. Though we were sometimes dark, we are now light in the Lord, so help us to walk as children of the light, proving what is acceptable unto the Lord. Though we were once not the people of God, now, through your mercy we have become the People of God so teach us to keep from evil and sin and not to yield our members as instruments of unrighteousness, but to yield ourselves unto God as those that are alive from the dead and our members as instruments of righteousness unto God, through Christ Jesus by the power of His Holy Spirit, Amen.

(a) Matt. 11: 28-30; Luke 24: 46-48; 1 Cor. 6: 11; Tit. 3: 3-7. (b) John 9: 41; John 15: 22. (c) John 17: 3; Acts 4: 12; Acts 10: 43. (d) Eph. 5: 8- 11; 1 Pet. 2: 9,10; Rom. 6: 1,2,12,13.

DAY 3: THE MISERY OF MAN

Question 6: Did God then create man so wicked and perverse?

Answer: By no means; but God created man good, (a) and after his own image, (b) in true righteousness and holiness, that he might rightly know God his Creator, heartily love him and live with him in eternal happiness to glorify and praise him. (c)

(a) Gen. 1: 31. (b) Gen. 1: 26,27. (c) Col. 3: 9,10; Eph. 4: 23,24; 2 Cor. 3: 18.

Question 7: Whence then proceeds this depravity of human nature?

Answer: From the fall and disobedience of our first parents, Adam and Eve, in Paradise; (a) hence our nature is become so corrupt, that we are all conceived and born in sin. (b)

(a) Gen. 3; Rom. 5: 12,18,19. (b) Ps. 51: 5; Gen. 5: 3.

Question 8: Are we then so corrupt that we are wholly incapable of doing any good, and inclined to all wickedness?

Answer: Indeed we are; (a) except we are regenerated by the Spirit of God. (b)

(a) Gen. 8: 21; John 3: 6; Gen. 6: 5; Job 14: 4; Job 15: 14,16,36; Isa. 53: 6. (b) John 3: 3,5; 1 Cor. 12: 3; 2 Cor. 3: 5.

Gracious God, by the Words of Your most Holy Law, no flesh is justified and we all lie in misery for our many sins, both those we have done in secret and those in the open. By Your Word came the knowledge of our sin and by it our misery. We have not loved you with all our heart, all our soul, all our mind or all our strength. We have hated our neighbor when we should have loved them. By our determined disobedience we have rejected Thy Law. We readily acknowledge that there is none righteous and by the deeds of the law, none can be justified. We have sinned and continue to fall short of your Glory. We reject the notion that we have not sinned and recognize that we are continually rebellious against Your Law. We recognize that we are often carnally minded, disobedient, deceived, malicious and our hearts are deceitful above all things. I see a law in my members which war against the law of my mind and bring me into captivity to the law of sin. Though you created us good and after your own image, in true righteousness and holiness, our first parents fell into disobedience and corrupted all of us so that we are all conceived and born in sin.

Because of the greatness of the Fall, only those who are regenerated by the Spirit of God, born of the Spirit, can one be saved. Jesus taught us that unless a man is born again, he cannot even see the Kingdom of God, let alone, long to belong again as a child of God. We beseech Thee, then, for mercy, that you would redeem us from under the curse of the Law and free us by your declaration of justified by faith alone in Christ alone according to the Scriptures alone through your Sovereign Grace alone. Amen.

4 GOD'S JUSTICE

Question 9: Does not God then do injustice to man, by requiring from him in his law, that which he cannot perform?

Answer: Not at all; (a) for God made man capable of performing it; but man, by the instigation of the devil, (b) and his own willful disobedience, (c) deprived himself and all his posterity of those divine gifts.

(a) Eph. 4: 24; Eccl. 7: 29. (b) John 8: 44; 2 Cor. 11: 3; Gen. 3: 4. (c) Gen. 3: 6; Rom. 5: 12; Gen. 3: 13; 1 Tim. 2: 13,14.

Question 10: Will God suffer such disobedience and rebellion to go unpunished?

Answer: By no means; but is terribly displeased (a) with our original as well as actual sins; and will punish them in his just judgment temporally and eternally, (b) as he has declared, "Cursed is every one that continueth not in all things, which are written in the book of the law, to do them." (c)

(a) Gen. 2: 17 ; Rom. 5: 12 . (b) Ps. 5: 5; Ps. 50: 21 ; Nah. 1: 2; Exod. 20: 5; Exod. 34: 7; Rom. 1: 18; Eph. 5: 6; Heb. 9: 27. (c) Deut. 27: 26; Gal. 3: 10.

Question 11: Is not God then also merciful?

Answer: God is indeed merciful, (a) but also just; (b) therefore his justice requires, that sin which is committed against the most high majesty of God, be also punished with extreme, that is, with everlasting punishment of body and soul.

(a) Exod. 34: 6,7; Exod. 20: 6. (b) Ps. 7: 9; Exod. 20: 5; Exod. 23: 7; Exod. 34: 7; Ps. 5: 5,6; Nah. 1: 2,3.

Almighty and Holy Lord, You have not been unjust to demand from your creatures that they follow your Law. Our inability to obey stems from our hatred of You and Your Law. You made us capable of performing it, but we, by the instigation of the devil and our own willful disobedience, have rejected it. Only You, by Your mercy, can put a new man within us, created in righteousness and true holiness. Only You, by Your grace can justify us from our sins. We therefore confess, that our sins are many and burden us down, that apart from Your gracious work of redemption, we have no good thing in us. We know that you are terribly displeased with our original sin, because we have been conceived in iniquity, as well as our actual sins, which are many. They rightfully deserve your temporal and eternal punishment for we are cursed because we have not continued in all things which are written in the book of your Law to do them.

But, you are also indeed merciful and just. Jesus Christ,

the Son of God, has stood in our stead, taking upon Himself the Justice we have deserved and satisfied for all the sins of Your People. LORD God Almighty, You alone are merciful, gracious, longsuffering and abundant in goodness and truth. You keep mercy for thousands, forgiving inquity and transgression and sins. Though you will not clear the guilty, yet, you visit mercy upon thousands of them that love Thee and keep your commands. God, you are a jealous God, yet Christ has taken upon Himself Your wrath against my sin and wickedness because You have loved me with an eternal love from before the foundations of the world. Help us to remember that we are dust and only because You have loved us first are we saved. Amen.

DAY 5: OF MAN'S DELIVERANCE

Question 12: Since then, by the righteous judgment of God, we deserve temporal and eternal punishment, is there no way by which we may escape that punishment, and be again received into favor?

Answer: God will have his justice satisfied: (a) and therefore we must make this full satisfaction, either by ourselves, or by another. (b)

(a) Gen. 2: 17; Exod. 20: 5; Exod. 23: 7; Ezek. 18: 4; Matt. 5: 26; 2 Thess. 1: 6; Luke 16: 2. (b) Rom. 8: 3,4.

Question 13: Can we ourselves then make this satisfaction?

Answer: By no means; but on the contrary we daily increase our debt. (a) (a). Job 9: 2,3; Job 15: 15,16; Job 4: 18,19; Ps. 130: 3; Matt. 6: 12; Matt. 18: 25; Matt. 16: 26.

Question 14: Can there be found anywhere, one, who is a mere creature, able to satisfy for us?

Answer: None; for, first, God will not punish any other creature for the sin which man has committed; (a) and further, no mere creature can sustain the burden of God's eternal wrath against sin, so as to deliver others from it. (b)

(a) Ezek. 18: 4; Gen. 3: 17; Heb. 2: 14-17. (b) Nah. 1: 6; Ps. 130: 3.

Question 15: What sort of a mediator and deliverer then must we seek for?

Answer: For one who is very man, and perfectly (a) righteous; (b) and yet more powerful than all creatures; that is, one who is also very God. (c)

(a) 1 Cor. 15: 21; Jer. 33: 16; Isa. 53: 9; 2 Cor. 5: 21. (b) Heb. 7: 16,26. (c) Isa. 7: 14; Isa. 9: 6; Rom. 9: 5; Jer. 23: 5,6; Jer. 23: 6; Luke 11: 22.

Lord God Almighty, because you are righteous and just, you will have your justice satisfied. However, we are sinners and can never make satisfaction for our own sins, let alone those of your People. Each day we increase our sins and know of a truth that man cannot be just with God apart from their sins being paid for. We drink iniquity like water, yea, even the heavens are not clean in your site. Yet, You promise that those who have placed their faith in the finished work of Christ will not have their iniquities marked against them. You have promised forgiveness to all who rely upon the righteousness and obedience of Jesus Christ, the Perfect God/Man. He is the one who took on Himself the nature and the seed of Abraham and is a merciful High Priest, who has reconciled His People to You. Apart from Christ, we could not stand before Your indignation, nor abide in the fierceness of Your anger. Oh Lord, if You should mark iniquities, O LORD, who could stand? Yet, though by one man, Adam, all humanity was plunged into sin and darkness, by One Man, Jesus Christ came also the resurrection of the dead. Your promise that in those days all Judah shall be saved has come about and will come about as You save your People. May we be numbered amongst the People of Israel for Christ has been made to be sin for us, who knew no sin, that we, might be made the righteousness of God in Him. We acknowledge that we have done no good deed but The LORD OUR RIGHTEOUSNESS is He who has declared us just, our sins satisfied by Jesus upon the Cross of Calvary. Because Jesus took upon Himself our sinful flesh, He, Who did not sin, by the Power of His Godhead, could sustain within his human nature the burden of God's wrath, so that He has obtained righteousness and life for His Own. By His Spirit, make us one of Your Own and apply to us His satisfaction for our sins thereby justifying us freely by your grace alone. Amen.

DAY 6: CHRIST OUR SUBSTITUTE

Question 16: Why must he be very man, and also perfectly righteous?

Answer: Because the justice of God requires that the same human nature which has sinned, should likewise make satisfaction for sin; (a) and one, who is himself a sinner, cannot satisfy for others. (b)

(a) Ezek. 18: 4,20; Rom. 5: 12,15,18; 1 Cor. 15: 21; Heb. 2: 14-16; 1 Pet. 3: 18; Isa .53: 3-5,10,11. (b) Heb. 7: 26,27; Ps. 49: 7,8; 1 Pet. 3: 18.

Question 17: Why must he in one person be also very God?

Answer: That he might, by the power of his Godhead (a) sustain in his human nature, (b) the burden of God's wrath; (c) and might obtain for, and restore to us, righteousness and life. (d)

(a) Isa. 9: 6; Isa. 63: 3. (b) Isa. 53: 4,11. (c) Deut. 4: 24; Nah. 1: 6; Ps. 130: 3. (d) Isa. 53: 5,11; Acts 2: 24; 1 Pet. 3: 18; John 3: 16; Acts 20: 28; John 1: 4.

Question 18: Who then is that Mediator, who is in one person both very God, (a) and a real (b) righteous man? (c)

Answer: Our Lord Jesus Christ: (d) "who of God is made unto us wisdom, and righteousness, and sanctification, and redemption." (e)

(a) 1 John 5: 20; Rom. 9: 5; Rom. 8: 3; Gal. 4: 4; Isa. 9: 6; Jer. 23: 6; Mal. 3: 1. (b) Luke 1: 42; Luke 2: 6,7; Rom. 1: 3; Rom. 9: 5; Philip. 2: 7; Heb. 2: 14,16,17; Heb. 4: 15. (c) Isa. 53: 9,11; Jer. 23: 5; Luke 1: 35; John 8: 46; Heb. 4: 15; Heb. 7: 26; 1 Pet. 1: 19; 1 Pet. 2: 22; 1 Pet. 3: 18. (d) 1 Tim. 2: 5; Heb. 2: 9; Matt. 1: 23; 1 Tim. 3: 16; Luke 2: 11. (e) 1 Cor. 1: 30.

Question 19: Whence knowest thou this?

Answer: From the holy gospel, which God himself first revealed in Paradise; (a) and afterwards published by the patriarchs (b) and prophets, (c) and represented by the sacrifices and other ceremonies of the law; (d) and lastly, has fulfilled it by his only begotten Son. (e)

(a) Gen. 3: 15. (b) Gen. 22: 18; Gen. 12: 3; Gen. 49: 10,11. (c) Isa. 53; Isa. 42: 1-4; Isa. 43: 25; Isa. 49: 5,6,22,23; Jer. 23: 5,6; Jer. 31: 32,33; Jer. 32: 39-41; Mic. 7: 18-20; Acts 10: 43; Rom. 1: 2; Heb. 1: 1; Acts 3: 22-24; Acts 10: 43; John 5: 46. (d) Heb. 10: 1,7; Col. 2: 7; John 5: 46. (e) Rom. 10: 4; Gal. 4: 4,5; Gal. 3: 24; Col. 2: 17.

Gracious, Heavenly Father, because Your justice requires that the same human nature which has sinned, should likewise make satisfaction for sin, and that no human can make that satisfaction because they have their own sins to answer for, You have graciously given us Your Son, the Incarnate Word of God, Blessed Second Person of the Holy Trinity, Jesus of Nazareth, to make satisfaction for the sins or your people of whom I am numbered. Because by man came death, so by man must also come the resurrection of the dead, and as much as Jesus was a partaker of flesh and blood, fully God and fully Man, the natures unmixed and no confusion, He, through His death on the cross has destroyed him that had the power of death, the devil and delivers those, who through fear of death where all our lifetime subject to bondage, He has suffered, once for our sins. He is the Just who took upon Himself the sins of the unjust, that He might bring us to God.

He is the High Priest of our souls and His suffering, once, for our sins, has quickened us by the Spirit so that we may be saved.

You have been faithful in granting the Promise given that a Child would be born who is the Mighty God, the Everlasting Father, the Prince of Peace. We have peace with You, Father, because of the Prince of Peace, our Brother, our Savior, Jesus Christ. He was wounded for our transgressions. It was He who was bruised for our iniquities; the chastisement of our peace landing upon the Innocent One for the guilty, and through His stripes we are healed of our sins. We are forever grateful that He purchased us, not with silver or gold, but the precious blood and makes us His own. He is the True God, the Eternal Life, God overall, blessed forever. Amen.

Nancy A. Almodovar

DAY 7: PARTICULAR REDEMPTION

Question 20: Are all men then, as they perished in Adam, saved by Christ?

Answer: No; (a) only those who are ingrafted into him, and, receive all his benefits, by a true faith. (b)

Isa. 53: 11; Ps. 2: 12; Rom. 11: 17,19,20; Rom. 3: 22; Heb. 4: 2,3; Heb. 5: 9; Heb. 10: 39; Heb. 11: 6.

Question 21: What is true faith?

Answer: True faith is not only a certain knowledge, whereby I hold for truth all that God has revealed to us in his word, (a) but also an assured confidence, (b) which the Holy Ghost (c) works by the gospel in my heart; (d) that not only to others, but to me also, remission of sin, everlasting righteousness and salvation, (e) are freely given by God, merely of grace, only for the sake of Christ's merits. (f)

(a) James 2: 19. (b) 2 Cor. 4: 13; Eph. 2: 7-9; Eph. 3: 12; Gal. 2: 16; Heb. 11: 1,7-10; Heb. 4: 16; James 1: 6; Matt. 16: 17; Philip. 1: 19; Rom. 4: 16-21; Rom. 5: 1; Rom. 1: 16; Rom. 10: 10,17; Rom. 3: 24.25. (c) Gal. 5: 22; Matt. 16: 17; 2 Cor. 4: 13; John 6: 29; Eph. 2: 8; Philip. 1: 19; Acts 16: 14. (d) Rom. 1: 16; Rom. 10: 17; 1 Cor. 1: 21; Acts 10: 44; Acts 16: 14. (e) Rom. 1: 17; Gal. 3: 11; Heb. 10: 10,38; Gal. 2: 16. (f) Eph. 2: 8; Rom. 3: 24; Rom. 5: 19; Luke 1: 77,78.

Question 22: What is then necessary for a Christian to believe?

Answer: All things promised us in the gospel, (a) which the articles of our catholic undoubted Christian faith briefly teach us.

(a) John 20: 31; Matt. 28: 19; Mark 1: 15.

Question 23: What are these articles?

Answer:

1. I believe in God the Father, Almighty, Maker of heaven and earth:

2. And in Jesus Christ, his only begotten Son, our Lord:

3. Who was conceived by the Holy Ghost, born of the Virgin Mary:

4. Suffered under Pontius Pilate; was crucified, dead, and buried: He descended into hell:

5. The third day he rose again from the dead:

6. He ascended into heaven, and sitteth at the right hand of God the Father Almighty:

7. From thence he shall come to judge the quick and the dead:

8. I believe in the Holy Ghost:

9. I believe a holy catholic church: the communion of saints:

10. The forgiveness of sins:

11. The resurrection of the body:

12. And the life everlasting.

Most Gracious Lord and Faithful Father, Only by your grace have we been ingrafted into Your Son, Jesus Christ, and through Him alone have we received all his benefits through true faith. By Your mercy alone you have granted us true faith, which believes in the Only One whom you sent to live and die on behalf of His People. By grace you have grafted us into that true tree, along with Abraham, which is of true faith. We who once were wide branches are now ingrafted into the People of God, who stand by faith no longer fearful. May your Gospel continue to be preached, as well unto those who are not yet known by You, as the Word was preached to us. Grant that it would be profitable to them being mixed with faith in them that hear it.

We know that true faith in you not only knows You by

the Written Word but believes all things Your Word teaches and contains. Grant us faith to receive all things which You teach us in the Scriptures, granting us gospel assurance and confidence by the Holy Spirit that our sins have been remitted and everlasting righteousness and salvation have been freely given by God to His People by grace for the sake of the merits of Christ alone. Grant that we will never look upon our faith as ours, but remember always it is a gift of grace from our Heavenly Father's Hand to His children; may we never look upon our works as good apart from the work of the Holy Spirit; may we never trust in ourselves but rather in the Rock Who is the sure foundation of our faith, the cornerstone of all Truth.

As Abraham was called out from among a pagan world, grant to us the mercy of being called out of this world and translated into the Kingdom of Light of Your Dear Son, Jesus Christ. May we remember that we are pilgrims and sojourners through this pagan land, here to proclaim Your Gospel amongst the world, while looking for a city which hath foundations, whose builder and maker is God.

Grant that because we belong to you, we will come boldly unto the throne of grace that we may obtain mercy and find grace to help in time of need.

May we cherish your Word, for these things are written that we might believe that Jesus is the Christ, the Son of God; and that believing we might have life through His Name. Amen.

DAY 8: THE ARTICLES OF OUR MOST HOLY FAITH

Question 24: How are these articles divided?

Answer: Into three parts; the first is of God the Father, and our creation; the second of God the Son, and our redemption; the third of God the Holy Ghost, and our sanctification.

Question 25: Since there is but one only divine essence, (a) why speakest thou of Father, Son, and Holy Ghost?

Answer: Because God has so revealed himself in his word, (b) that these three distinct persons are the one only true and eternal God.

(a) Deut. 6: 4; Eph. 4: 6; Isa. 44: 6; Isa. 45: 5; 1 Cor. 8: 4,6. (b) Isa. 61: 1; Luke 4: 18; Gen. 1: 2,3; Ps. 33: 6; Isa. 48: 16; Ps. 110: 1; Matt. 3: 16,17; Matt. 28: 19; 1 John 5: 7; Isa. 6: 1,3; John 14: 26; John 15: 26; 2 Cor. 13: 13; Gal. 4: 6; Eph. 2: 18; Tit. 3: 5,6.

ALMIGHTY and everlasting God, who hast given unto us thy servants grace, by the confession of a true faith, to acknowledge the glory of the eternal Trinity, and in the power of the Divine Majesty to worship the Unity; We beseech thee that thou wouldest keep us stedfast in this faith, and evermore defend us from all adversities, who livest and reignest, one God, world without end. OGOD, the strength of all those who put their trust in thee; Mercifully accept our prayers; and because, through the weakness of our mortal nature, we can do no good thing without thee, grant us the help of thy grace, that in keeping thy commandments we may please thee, both in will and deed; through Jesus Christ our Lord. *Amen.Amen.*

DAY 9: GOD OUR FATHER

Question 26: What believest thou when thou sayest, "I believe in God the Father, Almighty, Maker of heaven and earth"?

Answer: That the eternal Father of our Lord Jesus Christ (who of nothing made heaven and earth, with all that is in them; (a) who likewise upholds and governs the same by his eternal counsel and providence) (b) is for the sake of Christ his Son, my God and my Father; (c) on whom I rely so entirely, that I have no doubt, but he will provide me with all things necessary for soul and body (d) and further, that he will make whatever evils he sends upon me, in this valley of tears turn out to my advantage; (e) for he is able to do it, being Almighty God, (f) and willing, being a faithful Father. (g)

(a) Gen. 1,2; Job 33: 4; Job 38,39; Ps. 33: 6; Acts 4: 24; Acts 14: 15; Isa. 45: 7. (b) Matt. 10: 29; Heb. 1: 3; Ps. 104: 27- 30; Ps. 115: 3; Matt. 10: 29; Eph. 1: 11. (c) John 1: 12 ; Rom. 8: 15; Gal. 4: 5-7; Eph. 1: 5. (d) Ps. 55: 23; Matt. 6: 25,26; Luke 12: 22. (e) Rom. 8: 28. (f) Rom. 10: 12; Luke 12: 22; Rom. 8: 23; Isa. 46: 4; Rom. 10: 12. (g) Matt. 6: 25-34; Matt. 7: 9-11.

Gracious and ever loving God, we thank you that in Jesus Christ we can turn to you and call you 'Father', for you have adopted us into your family and made us one of your own children. Thank you that there is no going back on that and that our names are forever engraved on the palm of your hands. Come once more to draw us close to yourself, renewing in us the grace of repentance. Help us to turn away from anything that grieves you. Thus will you assure us of your steadfast love and restore in us the joy of your salvation, through our Lord Jesus Christ. Amen.

DAY 10: THE PROVIDENCE OF GOD

Question 27: What dost thou mean by the providence of God?

Answer: The almighty and everywhere present power of God; (a) whereby, as it were by his hand, he upholds and governs (b) heaven, earth, and all creatures; so that herbs and grass, rain and drought, (c) fruitful and barren years, meat and drink, health and sickness, (d) riches and poverty, (e) yea, and all things come, not by chance, but be his fatherly hand. (f)

(a) *Acts 17: 25-28; Jer. 23: 23,24; Isa. 29: 15,16; Ezek. 8: 12. (b) Heb. 1: 3. (c) Jer. 5: 24; Acts 14: 17. (d) John 9: 3. (e) Prov. 22: 2. (f) Matt. 10: 20; Prov. 16: 33.*

Question 28: What advantage is it to us to know that God has created, and by his providence does still uphold all things?

Answer: That we may be patient in adversity; (a) thankful in prosperity; (b) and that in all things, which may hereafter befall us, we place our firm trust in our faithful God and Father, (c) that nothing shall separate us from his love; (d) since all creatures are so in his hand, that without his will they cannot so much as move. (e)

(a) *Rom. 5: 3; James 1: 3; Ps. 39: 9; Job 1: 21,22. (b) Deut. 8: 10; 1 Thess. 5: 18. (c) Ps. 55: 22; Rom. 5: 4. (d) Rom. 8: 38,39. (e) Job 1: 12; Job 2: 6; Acts 17: 25,28; Prov. 21: 1.*

Heavenly Father, if I should suffer need, and go unclothed, and be in poverty, make my heart prize Thy love, know it, be constrained by it, though I be denied all blessings. It is Thy mercy to afflict and try me with wants, for by these trials I see my sins, and desire severance from them. Let me willingly accept misery, sorrows, temptations, if I can thereby feel sin as the greatest evil, and be delivered from it with gratitude to Thee, acknowledging this as the highest testimony of Thy Love.

O God, most high , most glorious, the thought of Your infinite serenity cheers me, for I am toiling and moiling, troubled and distressed, but You are forever at perfect peace. Your designs cause You no fear or care of unfulfilment, they stand fast as the eternal hills. Your power knows no bond, Your goodness no stint. You bring order out of confusion, and my defeats are Your victories: The Lord God omnipotent reigneth. I come to You as a sinner with cares and sorrows, to leave every concern entirely to You, every sin calling for Christ's precious blood; revive deep spirituality in my heart; let me live near to the great Shepherd, hear His voice, know its tones, follow its calls. Keep me from deception by causing me to abide in the truth, from harm by helping me to walk in the power of the Spirit. Give me intenser faith in the eternal verities, burning into me by experience the things I know; Let me never be ashamed of the truth of the gospel, that I may bear its reproach, vindicate it, see Jesus as its essence, know in it the power of the Spirit. Lord, help me, for I am often lukewarm and chill; unbelief mars my confidence, sin makes me forget You. Let the weeds that grow in my soul be cut at their roots; grant me to know that I truly live only when I live to You, that all else is trifling. Your presence alone can make me holy, devout, strong and happy. Abide in me, gracious God.

DAY 11: GOD THE SON

Question 29: Why is the Son of God called "Jesus", that is a Saviour?

Answer: Because he saveth us, and delivereth us from our sins; (a) and likewise, because we ought not to seek, neither can find salvation in any other. (b)

(a) Matt. 1: 21; Heb. 7: 24,25. (b) Acts 4: 12; John 15: 4,5; 1 Tim. 2: 5; Isa. 43: 11; 1 John 5: 11.

Question 30: Do such then believe in Jesus the only Saviour, who seek their salvation and welfare of saints, of themselves, or anywhere else?

Answer: They do not; for though they boast of him in words, yet in deeds they deny Jesus the only deliverer and Saviour; (a) for one of these two things must be true, that either Jesus is not a complete Saviour; or that they, who by a true faith receive this Saviour, must find all things in him necessary to their salvation. (b)

(a) 1 Cor. 1: 13,30,31; Gal. 5: 4. (b) Heb. 12: 2; Isa. 9: 6; Col. 1: 19,20; Col. 2: 10; 1 John 1: 7,16.

Gracious Father and Lord of All, In your infinite wisdom and divine plan you ordained that the Son of God would come down, clothed in flesh of our flesh and bone of our bone, incarnate and born of a virgin who would be called Jesus, for He would save His People from their sins, and continue forever, an unchangeable High Priest, where in His Name alone there would be salvation. Grant that we would abide in Him so that connected to the branch we would bear fruit for His honor. We thank you Jesus, that you are the only mediator between us and God and besides you there is no savior. Grant that we would seek our salvation only in you and that we would trust you alone for the welfare of all the saints throughout your world. May we boast of Jesus in all our works, worship Him as our sole source of righteousness and our only Savior. Amen.

DAY 12: JESUS THE CHRIST

Question 31: Why is he called "Christ", that is anointed?

Answer: Because he is ordained of God the Father, and anointed with the Holy Ghost, (a) to be our chief Prophet and Teacher, (b) who has fully revealed to us the secret counsel and will of God concerning our redemption; (c) and to be our only High Priest, (d) who by the one sacrifice of his body, has redeemed us, (e) and makes continual intercession with the Father for us; (f) and also to be our eternal King, who governs us by his word and Spirit, and who defends and preserves us in that salvation, he has purchased for us. (g)

(a) Heb. 1: 9; Ps. 45: 8; Isa. 61: 1; Luke 4: 18. (b) Deut. 18: 15; Acts 3: 22; Acts 7: 37; Isa. 55: 4. (c) John 1: 18; John 15: 15. (d) Ps. 110: 4. (e) Heb. 10: 12,14; Heb. 9: 12,14,28. (f) Rom. 8: 34; Heb .9: 24; 1 John 2: 1; Rom. 5: 9,10. (g) Ps. 2: 6; Zech. 9: 9; Matt. 21: 5; Luke 1: 33; Matt. 28: 18; John 10: 28; Rev. 12: 10,11.

Question 32: But why art thou called a Christian? (a)

Answer: Because I am a member of Christ by faith, (b) and thus am partaker of his anointing; (c) that so I may confess his name, (d) and present myself a living sacrifice of thankfulness to him: (e) and also that with a free and good conscience I may fight against sin and

Satan in this life (f) and afterwards I reign with him eternally, over all creatures. (g)

(a) Acts 11: 26. (b) 1 Cor. 6: 15. (c) 1 John 2: 27; Acts 2: 17. (d) Matt. 10: 32; Rom. 10: 10; Mark 8: 38. (e) Rom. 12: 1; 1 Pet. 2: 5,9; Rev. 5: 8,10; Rev. 1: 6. (f) 1 Pet. 2: 11; Rom. 6: 12,13; Gal. 5: 16,17; Eph. 6: 11; 1 Tim. 1: 18,19. (g) 2 Tim. 2: 12; Matt. 24: 34.

Gracious God and Heavenly Father, You ordain and anointed with the Holy God your Son, Jesus Christ, to be our Prophet and Teacher and He has fully revealed to us the secret counsel and will of God concerning our redemption. He has become our Only High Priest, who by the one sacrifice of his body, has redeemed us to be His own and as our High Priest continually makes intercession for us. We thank you that He is our Eternal King, who governs us by His written Word through the guidance of His Spirit and that He is our Defender, Preserver and Salvation. Most of all, we thank you that we belong to You because of Who Jesus Christ is. It is by Christ by faith that we too are partakers of His anointing so that we may confess His Name before the world. Grant us the desire and enable us to present ourselves a living sacrifice, pleasing to you, a life of thankfulness and a free and good conscience that we may fight against sin and satan in this life. May you preserve us in such a way that we bring you honor and glory both here and in the hereafter where we will reign with Him eternally over all creatures. Amen.

DAY 13: JESUS THE ONLY BEGOTTEN SON OF GOD

Question 33: Why is Christ called the "only begotten Son" of God, since we are also the children of God?

Answer: Because Christ alone is the eternal and natural Son of God; (a) but we are children adopted of God, by grace, for his sake. (b)

(a) John 1: 1-3,14,18; Heb. 1: 1,2; John 3: 16; 1 John 4: 9; Rom. 8: 32. (b) Rom. 8: 15-17; John 1: 12; Gal. 4: 6; Eph. 1: 5,6.

Question 34: Wherefore callest thou him "our Lord"?

Answer: Because he hath redeemed us, both soul and body, from all our sins, not with silver or gold, but with his precious blood, and has delivered us from all the power of the devil; and thus has made us his own property. (a)

(a) 1 Pet. 1: 18,19; 1 Pet. 2: 9; 1 Cor. 6: 20; 1 Cor. 7: 23; 1 Tim. 2: 6; John 20: 28.

We Praise Thee, Heavenly Father, that Christ is Thine
Only Begotten Son, Your one of a kind, only, sole and
unique Son, whom we confess with the Church of Old that
He is the only begotten Son of God,
begotten of his Father before all worlds,
God of God, Light of Light,
very God of very God,
begotten, not made,
being of one substance with the Father;

by whom all things were made;
who for us men and for our salvation
came down from heaven,
and was incarnate by the Holy Ghost
of the Virgin Mary,
and was made man;
and was crucified also for us under Pontius Pilate;
he suffered and was buried;
and the third day he rose again
according to the Scriptures,
and ascended into heaven,
and sitteth on the right hand of the Father;
and he shall come again, with glory,
to judge both the quick and the dead;
whose kingdom shall have no end.

This same Jesus, has redeemed us, both soul and body, from all our sins, not with silver or gold, but with his precious blood, and has delivered us from all the power of the devil. He has made us his own property and we rightly call Him Lord and Master. May we be that chosen generation, royal priesthood, a holy nation, peculiar people, so that we would show forth the praises of Thy Glory because You called us out of darkness into His marvelous light. Amen.

DAY 14: BORN OF A VIRGIN

Question 35: What is the meaning of these words "He was conceived by the Holy Ghost, born of the virgin Mary"?

Answer: That God's eternal Son, who is, and continues (a) true and eternal God, (b) took upon him the very nature of man, of the flesh and blood of the virgin Mary, (c) by the operation of the Holy Ghost; (d) that he might also be the true seed of David, (e) like unto his brethren in all things, (f) sin excepted. (g)

(a) Rom. 1: 4; Rom. 9: 5. (b) 1 John 5: 20; John 1: 1; John 17: 3; Rom. 1: 3; Col. 1: 15. (c) Gal. 4: 4; Luke 1: 31,42,43. (d) John 1: 14; Matt. 1: 18,20; Luke 1: 32,35. (e) Ps. 132: 11; Rom. 1: 3; 2 Sam. 7: 12; Acts 2: 30. (f) Philip. 2: 7; Heb. 2: 14,17. (g) Heb. 4: 15.

Question 36: What profit dost thou receive by Christ's holy conception and nativity?

Answer: That he is our Mediator; (a) and with His innocence and perfect holiness, covers in the sight of God, my sins, wherein I was conceived and brought forth. (b)

(a) Heb. 7: 26,27; Heb. 2: 17. (b) 1 Pet. 1: 18,19; 1 Pet. 3: 18; 1 Cor. 1: 30,31; Rom. 8: 3,4; Isa. 53: 11; Ps. 32: 1.

Lord God Almighty, We thank you that Your eternal Son, who was and is and is to come, eternal and true God, took upon Himself the flesh and blood of the virgin Mary, that He might be numbered among His brethren, we your People. We marvel at the mystery which is the incarnation, how your Holy Spirit overshadowed your servant Mary so that He was of the true seed of David, just as you promised of old through the prophets spoke. We gaze in wonder at God becoming flesh so that He may be like us in all things except sin. Because Jesus took our flesh upon Himself, He is rightfully our Mediator, standing

We pray with the Church of Old: ALMIGHTY God, who hast given us thy only. begotten Son to take our nature upon him, and as at this time to be born of a pure virgin*; Grant that we being regenerate, and made thy children by adoption and grace, may daily be renewed by thy holy† Spirit; through the same our Lord Jesus Christ, who liveth and reigneth with thee and the same Spirit ever, one God, world without end. *Amen.*. (*Book of Common Prayer, The Collect, The Nativity of our Lord, 1789 Edition*)

DAY 15: SUFFERING SERVANT

Question 37: What dost thou understand by the words, "He suffered"?

Answer: That he, all the time that he lived on earth, but especially at the end of his life, sustained in body and soul, the wrath of God against the sins of all mankind: (a) that so by his passion, as the only propitiatory sacrifice, (b) he might redeem our body and soul from everlasting damnation, (c) and obtain for us the favor of God, righteousness and eternal life. (d)

(a) Isa. 53: 4; 1 Pet. 2: 24; 1 Pet. 3: 18; 1 Tim. 2: 6. (b) Isa. 53: 10,12; Eph. 5: 2; 1 Cor. 5: 7; 1 John 2: 2; 1 John 4: 10; Rom. 3: 25; Heb. 9: 28; Heb. 10: 14. (c) Gal. 3: 13; Col. 1: 13; Heb. 9: 12; 1 Pet. 1: 18,19. (d) Rom. 3: 25; 2 Cor. 5: 21; John 3: 16; John 6: 51; Heb. 9: 15; Heb. 10: 19.

Question 38: Why did he suffer "under Pontius Pilate, as judge"?

Answer: That he, being innocent, and yet condemned by a temporal judge, (a) might thereby free us from the severe judgement of God to which we were exposed. (b)

(a) John 18: 38; Matt. 27: 24; Acts 4: 27,28; Luke 23: 14,15; John 19: 4. (b) Ps. 69: 4; Isa. 53: 4,5; 2 Cor. 5: 21; Gal. 3: 13.

Question 39: Is there anything more in his being "crucified", than if he had died some other death?

Answer: Yes there is; for thereby I am assured, that he took on him the curse which lay upon me; (a) for the death of the cross was accursed of God. (b)

(a) Gal. 3: 13. (b) Deut. 21: 23.

Gracious Father and God over all, Today we are reminded that Christ came and suffered all His life and in death for the sins of His people to be a propitiation for our sins and also for the sins of the whole world. Herein we see what love truly is, not that we loved You, Lord, but that You have loved us by offering once Your Only Son to bear the sins of many for those who look to Him for their salvation and redemption. We remember that He suffered, the righteous for the unrighteous and thank you that we were not redeemed with corruptible things but with the precious blood of Christ, as of a lamb without blemish and without spot. Thank you, that in your love and mercy, you, Lord Jesus, being innocent were condemned by a temporal judge that you might free us from the sever judgment of the Eternal judge to who's judgment we were exposed all our days. Your word said that anyone who hanged on a tree is "accursed of God" and yet, Lord Jesus, you willingly became a curse so that we might be redeemed and that the charges against us would be satisfied in your punishment upon the Cross of Calvary on the Hill of Golgotha. Because you have redeemed us from the curse of the law, we are saved. Remind us this day, when tempted to sin, that we are to live in righteousness because you are our righteousness. Amen.

DAY 16: HUMBLED UNTO DEATH

Question 40: Why was it necessary for Christ to humble himself even "unto death"?

Answer: Because with respect to the justice and truth of God, (a) satisfaction for our sins could be made no otherwise, than by the death of the Son of God. (b)

(a) Gen. 2: 17. (b) Rom. 8: 3,4; Heb. 2: 9,14,15.

Question 41: Why was he also "buried"?

Answer: Thereby to prove that he was really dead. (a)

(a) Matt. 27: 59,60; Luke 23: 52,53; John 19: 38-42; Acts 13: 29.

Question 42: Since then Christ died for us, why must we also die?

Answer: Our death is not a satisfaction for our sins, (a) but only an abolishing of sin, and a passage into eternal life. (b)

(a) Mark 8: 37; Ps. 49: 7. (b) John 5: 24; Philip. 1: 23; Rom. 7: 24.

Question 43: What further benefit do we receive from the sacrifice and death of Christ on the cross?

Answer: That by virtue thereof, our old man is crucified, dead and buried with him; (a) that so the corrupt inclinations of the flesh may no more reign in us; (b) but that we may offer ourselves unto him a sacrifice of thanksgiving. (c)

(a) Rom. 6: 6. (b) Rom. 6: 6-8,11,12; Col. 2: 12. (c) Rom. 12: 1.

Question 44: Why is there added, "he descended into hell"?

Answer: That in my greatest temptations, I may be assured, and wholly comfort myself in this, that my Lord Jesus Christ, by his inexpressible anguish, pains, terrors, and hellish agonies, in which he was plunged during all his sufferings, (a) but especially on the cross, has delivered me from the anguish and torments of hell. (b)

(a) Ps. 18: 5,6; Ps. 116: 3; Matt. 26: 38; Heb. 5: 7; Isa. 53: 10; Matt. 27: 46. (b) Isa. 53: 5.

God, You are a Holy God of Infinite Justice and Mercy, You, in your grace, sent your Only Begotten Son so that He would pay for all the sins of Your People because satisfaction for our sins could never be paid by any mere mortal nor any creature under heaven. Indeed, he was truly dead as evidence by his burial in the tomb unto the third day, and by that death we live. Even though we must still die, it is not a judgment against us, but you have made death the final abolishing of sin in us so that we may live eternally with you. We praise you that by virtue of Christ's death on the cross and sacrifice for our sins, that we are assured and comforted that Jesus Christ is mine and I am His, that by His pains, terrors and hellish agonies, He delivered us from the anguish and torments of hell. May we remember this as we travel through this earthly sod on the way to glory. Amen.

DAY 17: RAISED WITH CHRIST

Question 45: What does the "resurrection" of Christ profit us?

Answer: First, by his resurrection he has overcome death, that he might make us partakers of that righteousness which he had purchased for us by his death; (a) secondly, we are also by his power raised up to a new life; (b) and lastly, the resurrection of Christ is a sure pledge of our blessed resurrection. (c)

(a) 1 Cor. 15: 16; Rom. 4: 25; 1 Pet. 1: 3. (b) Rom. 6: 4; Col. 3: 1,3; Eph. 2: 5,6. (c) 1 Cor. 15: 12,20,21; Rom. 8: 11.

Ursinus, Zacharias (2012-12-18). The Heidelberg Catechism (Kindle Locations 440-441). . Kindle Edition.

Great God and Savior, through Whom we have redemption, To the Risen Christ, our Lord and Savior Jesus Christ, by your resurrection you have made us partakers of that righteousness who You purchased for us by Your death. Because You have been raised, we are comforted that we too, by the Power of Your Holy Spirit, has raised us from spiritual death to a new life in Your Son and that we have received the sure pledge that we too shall be raised incorruptible. Help us, by the power of Your Holy Spirit to so live today that we seek those things which are above, where Christ is seated on the right hand of God. Remind us, as we live in this vale of tears, that we are dead and our life is hid with Christ in God, so that we live in a manner worthy of our Savior, Jesus Christ. Ever remind us that our hope is grounded in the blessed truth that just as the Spirit of God raised up Jesus from the dead, so shall He also quicken our mortal bodies on that Great Day. Amen.

DAY 18: ASCENDED TO HEAVEN

Question 46: How dost thou understand these words, "he ascended into heaven"?

Answer: That Christ, in sight of his disciples, was taken up from earth into heaven; (a) and that he continues there for our interest, (b) until he comes again to judge the quick and the dead. (c)

(a) Acts 1: 9; Matt. 26: 64; Mark 16: 19; Luke 24: 51. (b) Heb. 7: 25; Heb. 4: 14; Heb. 9: 24; Rom. 8: 34; Eph. 4: 10; Col. 3: 1. (c) Acts 1: 11; Matt. 24: 30.

Question 47: Is not Christ then with us even to the end of the world, as he has promised? (a)

Answer: Christ is very man and very God; with respect to his human nature, he is no more on earth; (b) but with respect to his Godhead, majesty, grace and spirit, he is at no time absent from us. (c)

(a) Matt. 28: 20. (b) Heb. 8: 4; Matt. 26: 11; John 16: 28; John 17: 11; Acts 3: 21. (c) John 14: 17-19; John 16: 13; Matt. 28: 20; Eph. 4: 8,12.

Question 48: But if his human nature is not present, wherever his Godhead is, are not then these two natures in Christ separated from one another?

Answer: Not as all, for since the Godhead is illimitable and omnipresent, (a) it must necessarily follow that the same is beyond the limits of the human nature he assumed, (b) and yet is nevertheless in this human nature, and remains personally united to it.

(a) Acts 7: 49; Jer. 23: 24. (b) Col. 2: 9; John 3: 13; John 11: 15; Matt. 28: 6.

Question 49: Of what advantage to us is Christ's ascension into heaven?

Answer: First, that he is our advocate in the presence of his Father in heaven; (a) secondly, that we have our flesh in heaven as a sure pledge that he, as the head, will also take up to himself, us, his members; (b) thirdly, that he sends us his Spirit as an earnest, (c) by whose power we "seek the things which are above, where Christ sitteth on the right hand of God, and not things on earth." (d)

(a) 1 John 2: 1; Rom. 8: 34. (b) John 14: 2; John 17: 24; John 20: 17; Eph. 2: 6. (c) John 14: 16,7; Acts 2: 1-4,33; 2 Cor. 1: 22; 2 Cor. 5: 5. (d) Col. 3: 1; Philip. 3: 14.

Our Living God and Risen Lord, Jesus Christ, by the Grace and mercy of our Heavenly Father, you were raised from the dead and ascended from earth into heaven. There, you continue on our behalf, for our interest, until you come again to judge the living and the dead. Yet, you have promise to be with us even to the end of the world and as both God and Man, You remain with us by Your Spirit and are seated at the right hand of God Almighty where you ever live to make intercession for us. Just as you promise that you are with us always, even to the end of the world, you also dwell with the Father and the Holy Spirit, blessed Trinity. You have not left us comfortless and continue, by your Spirit to teach us to observe all things.

DAY 19: ASCENDED TO HEAVEN

Question 50: Why is it added, "and sitteth at the right hand of God"?

Answer: Because Christ is ascended into heaven for this end, that he might appear as head of his church, (a) by whom the Father governs all things. (b)

(a) Eph. 1: 20,21,23; Col. 1: 18. (b) Matt. 28: 18; John 5: 22.

Question 51: What profit is this glory of Christ, our head, unto us?

Answer: First, that by his Holy Spirit he pours out heavenly graces upon us his members; (a) and then that by his power he defends and preserves us against all enemies. (b)

(a) Acts 2: 33; Eph. 4: 8. (b) Ps. 2: 9; Ps. 110: 1,2; John 10: 28; Eph. 4: 8.

Question 52: What comfort is it to thee that "Christ shall come again to judge the quick and the dead"?

Answer: That in all my sorrows and persecutions, with uplifted head I look for the very same person, who before offered himself for my sake, to the tribunal of God, and has removed all curse from me, to come as judge from heaven: (a) who shall cast all his and my enemies into everlasting condemnation, (b) but shall translate me with all his chosen ones to himself, into heavenly joys and glory. (c)

(a) Luke 21: 28; Rom. 8: 23; Philip. 3: 20; Tit. 2: 13; 1 Thess. 4: 16. (b) 2 Thess. 1: 6,8-10; Matt. 25: 41-43. (c) Matt. 25: 34; 2 Thess. 1: 7.

Gracious Heavenly Father, Thank you that because Christ has ascended and now sits at Your right hand, so that He may appear before you on behalf of your People the Church, thank you that He has poured out heavenly grace upon us by His Holy Spirit and so defend and preserves us against all our enemies that in our sorrows and persecutions we may with uplifted head look for the very same Person, who before offered Himself for our sake to the your tribunal, standing before Your judgment seat as our Substitute and Satisfaction for our sins. Thank you that He has removed all curse from us and will cast all our enemies into everlasting condemnation but will translate me with all His Chosen Ones to Himself and into heavenly joys and glory. We deserve none of this, but for His sake, You have declared us just our sins having been satisfied by Your Only Begotten Son. Help us to live in the glorious truth of our freedom so that we may live unto you in a manner which reflects to others the mercy we have received at Your Hand. Amen.

DAY 20: OF GOD THE HOLY GHOST

Question 53: What dost thou believe concerning the Holy Ghost?

Answer: First, that he is true and coeternal God with the Father and the Son; (a) secondly, that he is also given me, (b) to make me by a true faith, partaker of Christ and all his benefits, (c) that he may comfort me (d) and abide with me for ever. (e)

(a) 1 John 5: 7; Gen. 1: 2; Isa. 48: 16; 1 Cor. 3: 16; 1 Cor. 6: 19; Acts 5: 3,4. (b) Gal. 4: 6; Matt. 28: 19,20; 2 Cor. 1: 21,22; Eph. 1: 13. (c) Gal. 3: 14; 1 Pet. 1: 2; 1 Cor. 6: 17. (d) Acts 9: 31; John 15: 26. (e) John 14: 16; 1 Pet. 4: 14.

God in Three Persons, Blessed Trinity, we know that the earth was voice and without form until the Spirit of God moved upon the faces of the waters, that nothing existed until God spoke and there was light. He alone, who spoke everything into being by His Word through His Spirit, has called us into His Light and Holy Spirit You now dwell in us and have made us temples of Yourself. We dare not lie to you as Ananias and Sapphira did for You are the Lord God who is Thrice Holy. You have granted us the honor to call God Father, Abba Father and it is in His Name, Father Son and Holy Spirit into whom we have been baptized. You have sealed us and given us the earnest of our salvation, that promise of eternal life which began when you regenerated us while we were yet dead in our sins and trespasses. You, Holy Spirit, have joined us unto the Lord in one Spirit and have comforted your Church through all the ages from the days of Seth to the last child of election is called. Jesus Christ, you promised us that the Spirit would guide us into all truth and we ask that He Who proceeds from the Father will continue to testify of the Christ, the Son of the Living God through your Word as it is proclaimed and read. Grant us grace, that if reproached for the name of Christ we will be happy for the Spirit of glory and of God rests upon us so that He might be glorified in all things. Amen.

DAY 21: THE HOLY CATHOLIC CHURCH

Question 54: What believest thou concerning the "holy catholic church" of Christ?

Answer: That the Son of God (a) from the beginning to the end of the world, (b) gathers, defends, and preserves (c) to himself by his Spirit and word, (d) out of the whole human race, (e) a church chosen to everlasting life, (f) agreeing in true faith; (g) and that I am and forever shall remain, (h) a living member thereof. (i)

(a) Eph. 5: 26; John 10: 11; Acts 20: 28; Eph. 4: 11-13. (b) Ps. 71: 17,18; Isa. 59: 21; 1 Cor. 11: 26. (c) Matt. 16: 18; John 10: 28-30; Ps. 129: 1-5. (d) Isa. 59: 21; Rom. 1: 16; Rom. 10: 14-17; Eph. 5: 26. (e) Gen. 26: 4; Rev. 5: 9. (f) Rom. 8: 29,30; Eph. 1: 10-13. (g) Acts 2: 46; Eph. 4: 3-6. (h) Ps. 23: 6; 1 Cor. 1: 8,9; John 10: 28; 1 John 2: 19; 1 Pet. 1: 5. (i) 1 John 3: 14,19-21; 2 Cor. 13: 5; Rom. 8: 10.

Question 55: What do you understand by "the communion of saints"?

Answer: First, that all and every one, who believes, being members of Christ, are in common, partakers of him, and of all his riches and gifts; (a) secondly, that every one must know it to be his duty, readily and cheerfully to employ his gifts, for the advantage and salvation of other members. (b)

(a) 1 John 1: 3; 1 Cor. 1: 9; Rom. 8: 32; 1 Cor. 12: 12,13; 1 Cor. 6: 17. (b) 1Cor. 12: 21; 1 Cor. 13: 1,5; Philip. 2: 4-8.

Question 56: What believest thou concerning "the forgiveness of sins"?

Answer: That God, for the sake of Christ's satisfaction, will no more remember my sins, neither my corrupt nature, against which I have to struggle all my life long; (a) but will graciously impute to me the righteousness of Christ, (b) that I may never be condemned before the tribunal of God. (c)

(a) 1 John 2: 2; 1 John 1: 7; 2 Cor. 5: 19,21. (b) Jer. 31: 34; Ps. 103: 3,4; Ps. 103: 10,12; Mic. 7: 19,23-25. (c) Rom. 8: 1-4; John 3: 18; John 5: 24.

Blessed Father and LORD, from the beginning of the world to it's end, you have by Your Son gathered and continue to gather, defend, preserve to yourself by Your Spirit and Word, out of the whole human race, a church chosen to everlasting life. This Church agreeing in true faith, I am and forever shall remain a living member thereof. You have sanctified and cleansed Your Church, your People by the washing of water by the Word; You are the Good Shepherd who gave His life for the Sheep; Blessed Holy Spirit, You watch over the flock of God, so we pray that your overseers will feed the Church which Christ purchased with His own blood. You, Christ, when you asked St. Peter who you are, promised that You will build Your Church so that the gates of Hell will not prevail against Her. We pray, give life to all whom you call, preserve them so that none can pluck them out of your hand for The LORD is our righteousness. Let those who hate your Church, who hate Zion Your People from among both Jew and Gentile, be confounded. We pray, do not take your Spirit from your Church but keep the covenant with them. Make the proclamation of Your gospel the power of God unto salvation; let it not go without fruit from the pulpit and keep our preachers and ministers of Word and Sacrament faithful in all thing, protecting them as they fend off the wolves and feed the saints.

May all who believe, being members of Christ, have

common participation in Him and all His riches and gifts, so that we may know our duty and readily and cheerfully employ our gifts for the advantage and salvation of other members of Your Body, the Church, the People of God, the True Israel.

May we daily remember that God, for the sake of Christ's satisfaction, you will no more remember our sins, neither our corrupt natures against which we struggle all our lives long; may you graciously impute to us the righteousness of Christ that we will never be condemned before the tribunal of God. Forgive us our sins and remember our trespasses no more. Amen.

DAY 22: RAISED WITH CHRIST

Question 57: What comfort does the "resurrection of the body" afford thee?

Answer: That not only my soul after this life shall be immediately taken up to Christ its head; (a) but also, that this my body, being raised by the power of Christ, shall be reunited with my soul, and made like unto the glorious body of Christ. (b)

(a) Luke 16: 22; Luke 23: 43; Philip. 1: 21,23. (b) 1 Cor. 15: 53,54; Job 19: 25,26; 1 John 3: 2; Philip. 3: 21.

Question 58: What comfort takest thou from the article of "life everlasting"?

Answer: That since I now feel in my heart the beginning of eternal joy, (a) after this life, I shall inherit perfect salvation, which "eye has not seen, nor ear heard, neither has it entered into the heart of man" to conceive, and that to praise God therein for ever. (b)

(a) 2 Cor. 5: 2,3. (b) 1 Cor. 2: 9; John 17: 3.

Gracious and Merciful Father, who remembers our sins no more because of the Righteousness of Your Beloved Son, our Savior, Jesus Christ, comfort us in the knowledge that after this life we will be immediately taken up to Christ who is our Head and that this body will be raised too by the power of Christ and be reunited with our souls and made like unto the glorious body of Christ. Comfort your people with the knowledge that since we now feel in our hearts the beginning of eternal joy, after this life, we shall inherit perfect salvation, which "eye has not seen, nor ear heard, neither has it entered into the hear of man" to conceive what awaits Your People and that we shall praise God for this promise of eternal life which has begun here below and will be perfected in Heaven.

DAY 23: WHY SUCH FAITH?

Question 59: But what does it profit thee now that thou believest all this?

Answer: That I am righteous in Christ, before God, and an heir of eternal life. (a)

(a) Hab. 2: 4; Rom. 1: 17; John 3: 36.

Question 60: How are thou righteous before God?

Answer: Only by a true faith in Jesus Christ; (a) so that, though my conscience accuse me, that I have grossly transgressed all the commandments of God, and kept none of them, (b) and am still inclined to all evil; (c) notwithstanding, God, without any merit of mine, (d) but only of mere grace, (e) grants and imputes to me, (f) the perfect satisfaction, (g) righteousness and holiness of Christ; (h) even so, as if I never had had, nor committed any sin: yea, as if I had fully accomplished all that obedience which Christ has accomplished for me; (i) inasmuch as I embrace such benefit with a believing heart. (j)

(a) Rom. 3: 21-25,28; Rom. 5: 1,2; Gal. 2: 16; Eph. 2: 8,9; Philip. 3: 9. (b) Rom. 3: 9. (c) Rom. 7: 23. (d) Tit. 3: 5; Deut. 9: 6; Ezek. 36: 22. (e) Rom. 3: 24; Eph. 2: 8. (f) Rom. 4: 4,5; 2 Cor. 5: 19. (g) 1 John 2: 2. (h) 1 John 2: 1. (i) 2 Cor. 5: 21. (j) Rom. 3: 22; John 3: 18.

Question 61: Why sayest thou, that thou art righteous by faith only?

Answer: Not that I am acceptable to God, on account of the worthiness of my faith; but because only the satisfaction, righteousness, and holiness of Christ, is my righteousness before God; (a) and that I cannot receive and apply the same to myself any other way than by faith only. (b)

(a) 1 Cor. 1: 30; 1 Cor. 2: 2. (b) 1 John 5: 10.

Merciful Father, Some would ask us why we believe in You, why this faith? But this faith does not come from within us through our own power, it is a gracious gift you have given us unto eternal life. You have declared us righteous for You have said, "The just shall live by faith". Because You have granted us saving faith, believing on the Son we have everlasting life.

Only by a true faith in Jesus Christ are we now righteous and you have granted us this assurance so that though our conscience accuse us, though we grossly transgress all the commandments you have given us, we have kept none of them, are still inclined to all evil; notwithstanding, You, God and Father, without any merit of ours but only of mere grace, you have granted and imputes to us, your People, the perfect satisfaction, righteousness and holiness of Christ; You have mercifully declared that we had never had nor committed any sin, yes, even that we have fully accomplished all that obedience which in actuality Christ accomplished for us. Inasmuch as we embrace these truths, we receive your justification through a believing heart.

With Martin Luther we pray "Lord Jesus, You are our righteousness and we are your sin. You have taken upon yourself what is ours and given us what is yours."

Never would we say this faith comes from ourselves, for we know that we are acceptable to God, not on account of the worthiness of our faith; but because only the satisfaction, righteousness, and holiness of Christ is our Righteousness before You and that we cannot receive and apply this righteousness in any other way other than by faith alone. Make us ever mindful of your mercy, your compassion, your exceeding kindness toward us sinners, throughout this day and for all our lives. Amen.

DAY 24: GOOD WORKS ARE NOT GOOD

Question 62: But why cannot our good works be the whole, or part of our righteousness before God?

Answer: Because, that the righteousness, which can be approved of before the tribunal of God, must be absolutely perfect, (a) and in all respects conformable to the divine law; and also, that our best works in this life are all imperfect and defiled with sin. (b)

(a) Gal. 3: 10; Deut. 27: 26. (b) Isa. 64: 6.

Question 63: What! do not our good works merit,

which yet God will reward in this and in a future life?

Answer: This reward is not of merit, but of grace. (a)

(a) Luke 17: 10.

Question 64: But does not this doctrine make men careless and profane?

Answer: By no means: for it is impossible that those, who are implanted into Christ by a true faith, should not bring forth fruits of thankfulness. (a)

(a) Matt. 7: 18; John 15: 5.

Thrice Holy One, we know that Your Word says that we are all as an unclean thing, and all our righteousnesses are as filthy rags, that we all fade as a leaf; and our iniquities, like the wind, have taken us away. Your Word says that as many as are of the works of the law are under the curse for Cursed is everyone that continues not in all things which are written in the book of the law to do them. We, sinners by birth and by nature, are cursed and wretched.

But, praise be to Your Holy Name, you have not left us as such, but by grace alone, you have given us true faith, which looks to Christ alone for righteousness, obedience and satisfaction for your Law. We know our works do not merit your favor or kindness, neither in this life nor the next, for if we do good it is only the work of Christ by Your Holy Spirit in us and we are unprofitable servants only doing what is our duty to do. We thank you that because we have been born again, born of a new spirit, we should now bring forth works of thankfulness for it is impossible that those who have been implanted in Christ by true faith should not bring them forth to your glory and honor. Grant us this day that we bring forth fruits unto righteousness for it is You who work in us to both will and to do of your good pleasure. Amen.

DAY 25: MEANS OF GRACE: THE SACRAMENTS

Question 65: Since then we are made partakers of Christ and all his benefits by faith only, whence does this faith proceed?

Answer: From the Holy Ghost, (a) who works faith in our hearts by the preaching of the gospel, and confirms it by the use of the sacraments. (b)

(a) Eph. 2: 8,9; Eph. 6: 23; John 3: 5; Philip. 1: 29. (b) Matt. 28: 19,20; 1 Pet. 1: 22,23.

Question 66: What are the sacraments?

Answer: The sacraments are holy visible signs and seals, appointed of God for this end, that by the use thereof, he may the more fully declare and seal to us the promise of the gospel, viz., that he grants us freely the remission of sin, and life eternal, for the sake of that one sacrifice of Christ, accomplished on the cross. (a)

(a) Gen. 17: 11; Rom. 4: 11; Deut. 30: 6; Lev. 6: 25; Heb. 9: 7-9,24; Ezek. 20: 12; Isa. 6: 6,7; Isa. 54: 9.

Question 67: Are both word and sacraments, then, ordained and appointed for this end, that they may direct our faith to the sacrifice of Jesus Christ on the cross, as the only ground of our salvation? (a)

Answer: Yes, indeed: for the Holy Ghost teaches us in the gospel, and assures us by the sacraments, that the whole of our salvation depends upon that one sacrifice of Christ which he offered for us on the cross.

(a) Rom. 6: 3; Gal. 3: 27.

Question 68: How many sacraments has Christ instituted in the new covenant, or testament?

Answer: Two: namely, holy baptism, and the holy supper.

Faithful Father, You have not left your children without food and drink so that they may grow but you have granted us the preaching of the Gospel confirming it by the use of sacraments which we know are visible signs and seals, appointed by You that you may declare more fully to us that seal and promise of the Gospel: the forgiveness of sins and life eternal for the sake of Christ which was accomplished on the cross. It is both by word and signs and seals that you have ordained and appointed to teach us by the Holy Spirit in the gospel and assure us of our salvation that it depends upon Christ which He offered for us on the Cross. It is baptism and the Holy Supper which grants us the sign and seal of our salvation wrought by Your Son, through Whom we pray in thanksgiving, Amen.

DAY 26: HOLY BAPTISM

Question 69: How art thou admonished and assured by holy baptism, that the one sacrifice of Christ upon the cross is of real advantage to thee?

Answer: Thus: That Christ appointed this external washing with water, (a) adding thereto this promise, (b) that I am as certainly washed by his blood and Spirit from all the pollution of my soul, that is, from all my sins, (c) as I am washed externally with water, by which the filthiness of the body is commonly washed away.

(a) Matt. 28: 19. (b) Matt .28: 19; Acts 2: 38; Matt. 3: 11; Mark 16: 16; John 1: 33; Rom. 6: 3,4. (c) 1 Pet. 3: 21; Mark 1: 4; Luke 3: 3

Question 70: What is it to be washed with the blood and Spirit of Christ?

Answer: It is to receive of God the remission of sins, freely, for the sake of Christ's blood, which he shed for us by his sacrifice upon the cross; (a) and also to be renewed by the Holy Ghost, and sanctified to be members of Christ, that so we may more and more die unto sin, and lead holy and unblamable lives. (b)

(a) Heb. 12: 24; 1 Pet. 1: 2; Rev. 1: 5; Rev. 7: 14; Zech. 13: 1; Ezek. 36: 25. (b) John 1: 33; John 3: 5; 1 Cor. 6: 11; 1 Cor. 12: 13; Rom. 6: 4; Col. 2: 12.

Question 71: Where has Christ promised us, that he will as certainly wash us by his blood and Spirit, as we are washed with the water of baptism?

Answer: In the institution of baptism, which is thus expressed: "Go ye, therefore, and teach all nations, baptizing them in the name of the Father, and of the Son, and of the Holy Ghost", Matthew 28:19. And "he that believeth, and is baptized, shall be saved; but he that believeth not, shall be damned.", Mark 16:16. This promise is also repeated, where the scripture calls baptism "the washing of regenerations" and the washing away of sins.(a)

(a) Tit. 3: 5; Acts 22: 16.

God our Father, the Lord Jesus Christ admonished us to be baptized with the washing of water and by our baptism we know that the washing is not our promise to you, nor is it a public statement of our desire to follow you, but rather, it is a sign and seal you have given to the Church and to all who believe and their household. We thank you that as certainly as we are washed by His blood and Spirit from all pollution of our souls, from our sins, as much as water washes away the filthiness of the body, so too are we washed unto the forgiveness of our sins. Thank you that through our baptism, which is a sign and seal of the reality of Christ's blood and the washing of regeneration by the Holy Spirit we are renewed and set apart as members of Christ so that we may more and more die unto sin and lead holy and unblamable lives. We praise you that Christ has promised that He will wash us by his blood and Spirit as we are washed in the waters of baptism, in the Name of the Father, and of the Son and of the Holy Spirit, and he that believes will be saved but he that does not believe will be damned. Remind us daily of the promise that scripture calls baptism the washing of regeneration and the washing away of sins. Enable us to live this day in a manner which echoes to the world the promise You gave us at our baptism, mark us out again as belonging to you, as baptism marked us as one of Your Own. Amen.

DAY 27: WASHING AWAY OF SIN

Question 72: Is then the external baptism with water the washing away of sin itself?

Answer: Not at all: (a) for the blood of Jesus Christ only, and the Holy Ghost cleanse us from all sin. (b)

(a) Matt. 3: 11; 1 Pet. 3: 21; Eph. 5: 26,27. (b) 1 John 1: 7; 1 Cor. 6: 11.

Question 73: Why then does the Holy Ghost call baptism "the washing of regeneration," and "the washing away of sins"?

Answer: God speaks thus not without great cause, to-wit, not only thereby to teach us, that as the filth of the body is purged away by water, so our sins are removed by the blood and Spirit of Jesus Christ; (a) but especially that by this divine pledge and sign he may assure us, that we are spiritually cleansed from our sins as really, as we are externally washed with water. (b)

(a) Rev. 1: 5; Rev. 7: 14; 1 Cor. 6: 11. (b) Mark 16: 16; Gal. 3: 27.

Question 74: Are infants also to be baptized?

Answer: Yes: for since they, as well as the adult, are included in the covenant and church of God; (a) and since redemption from sin (b) by the blood of Christ, and the Holy Ghost, the author of faith, is promised to them no less than to the adult; (c) they must therefore by baptism, as a sign of the covenant, be also admitted into the Christian church; and be distinguished from the children of unbelievers (d) as was done in the old covenant or testament by circumcision, (e) instead of which baptism is instituted (f) in the new covenant.

(a) Gen. 17: 7. (b) Matt. 19: 14. (c) Luke 1: 15; Ps. 22: 10; Isa. 44: 1-3; Acts 2: 39. (d) Acts 10: 47. (e) Gen. 17: 14. (f) Col. 2: 11-13.

Merciful Lord, You do not speak without great cause, to wit, that not only do you teach us that as the filth of the body is purged away by water, so our sins are removed by the blood and Spirit of Jesus Christ, but especially that this baptism is the divine pledge and sign wherewith you assure us that we are spiritually cleaned from our sins, as really as we are externally washed with water. You have sanctified us by the washing of water by the Word so that you might present us to yourself a glorious church, not having spot, or wrinkle, or any such thing; but that we should be holy. You have made us a holy People by your Covenant of Grace. Remind us of the covenant promise made to those in our homes who received the mark but have wandered, draw them to Yourself and fulfill the promise in them as you have done with us. Amen.

DAY 28: THE HOLY SUPPER

Question 75: How art thou admonished and assured in the Lord's Supper, that thou art a partaker of that one sacrifice of Christ, accomplished on the cross, and of all his benefits?

Answer: Thus: That Christ has commanded me and all believers, to eat of this broken bread, and to drink of this cup, in remembrance of him, adding these promises: (a) first, that his body was offered and broken on the cross for me, and his blood shed for me, as certainly as I see with my eyes, the bread of the Lord broken for me, and the cup communicated to me; and further, that he feeds and nourishes my soul to everlasting life, with his crucified body and shed blood, as assuredly as I receive from the hands of the minister, and taste with my mouth the bread and cup of the Lord, as certain signs of the body and blood of Christ.

(a) Matt. 26: 26-28; Mark 14: 22-24; Luke 22: 19,20; 1 Cor. 10: 16,17; 1 Cor. 11: 23-25; 1 Cor. 12: 13.

Question 76: What is it then to eat the crucified body, and drink the shed blood of Christ?

Answer: It is not only to embrace with believing heart all the sufferings and death of Christ and thereby to obtain the pardon of sin, and life eternal; (a) but also, besides that, to become more and more united to his sacred body, (b) by the Holy Ghost, who dwells both in Christ and in us; so that we, though Christ is in heaven (c) and we on earth, are notwithstanding "flesh of his flesh and bone of his bone" (d) and that we live, and are governed forever by one spirit, (e) as members of the same body are by one soul.

(a) John 6: 35,40,47-54. (b) John 6: 55,56. (c) Col. 3: 1; Acts 3: 21; 1 Cor. 11: 26. (d) Eph. 3: 16; Eph. 5: 29,30,32; 1 Cor. 6: 15,17,19; 1 John 3: 24; 1 John 4: 13; John 14: 23. (e) John 6: 56-58; John 15: 1-6; Eph. 4: 15,16.

Question 77: Where has Christ promised that he will as certainly feed and nourish believers with his body and bleed, as they eat of this broken bread, and drink of this cup?

Answer: In the institution of the supper, which is thus expressed: (a) "The Lord Jesus, the same night in which he was betrayed, took bread, and when he had given thanks, he brake it, and: said: eat, this is my body, which is broken for you; this do in remembrance of me.

51

After the same manner also he took the cup, when he had supped, saying: this cup is the new testament in my blood; this do ye, as often as ye drink it, in remembrance of me. For, as often as ye eat this bread, and drink this cup, ye do show the Lord's death till he come." 1 Corinthians 11:23-26. This promise is repeated by the holy apostle Paul, where he says "The cup of blessing which we bless, is it not the communion of the blood of Christ? The bread which we break, is it not the communion of the body of Christ? For we being many are one bread, and one body: for we are all partakers of that one bread." 1 Corinthians 10:16,17.

(a) 1 Cor. 11: 23-25; Matt .26: 26-28; Mark 14: 22-24; Luke 22: 19,20; 1 Cor. 10: 16,17.

O Father of Mercy, and GOD of all consolation! Seeing all creatures do acknowledge and confess thee as Governor and LORD: It becometh us, the workmanship of thine own hands, at all times to reverence and magnify thy godly Majesty. First, for that thou hast created us in thine own image and similitude: But chiefly in that thou hast delivered us from that everlasting death and damnation, into the which Satan drew mankind by the means of sin, from the bondage whereof neither man nor angel was able to make us free.

We praise thee, O LORD! That thou, rich in mercy, and infinite in goodness, hast provided our redemption to stand in thine only and well-beloved Son, whom of very love thou didst give to be made man like unto us in all things, sin excepted, in his body to receive the punishment of our transgression, by his death to make satisfaction to thy justice, and through his resurrection to destroy him that was the author of death; and so to bring again life to the world, from which the whole offspring of Adam most justly was exiled.

O LORD! We acknowledge that no creature is able to

comprehend the length and breadth, the depth and height of that thy most excellent love, which moved thee to show mercy where none was deserved, to promise and give life where death had gotten the victory, to receive us in thy grace when we could do nothing but rebel against thy justice.

O LORD! The blind dullness of our corrupt nature will not suffer us sufficiently to weigh these thy most ample benefits; yet, nevertheless, at the commandment of JESUS CHRIST our Lord, we present ourselves at this his table, which he hath left to be used in remembrance of his death, until his coming again: to declare and witness before the world, that by him alone we have received liberty and life; that by him alone thou dost acknowledge us thy children and heirs; that by him alone we have entrance to the throne of thy grace; that by him alone we are possessed in our spiritual kingdom to eat and drink at his table, with whom we have our conversation presently in heaven, and by whom our bodies shall be raised up again from the dust, and shall be placed with him in that endless joy, which thou — O Father of Mercy! — hast prepared for thine elect before the foundation of the world was laid.

And these most inestimable benefits we acknowledge and confess to have received of thy free mercy and grace, by thine only beloved Son JESUS CHRIST: for the which, therefore, we thy congregation, moved by thine Holy Spirit, render all thanks, praise, and glory, for ever and ever. Amen. (Prayer by John Knox)

DAY 29: THE BREAD AND WINE

Question 78: Do then the bread and wine become the very body and blood of Christ?

Answer: Not at all: (a) but as the water in baptism is not

53

changed into the blood of Christ, neither is the washing away of sin itself, being only the sign and confirmation thereof appointed of God; (b) so the bread in the Lord's supper is not changed into the very body of Christ; (c) though agreeably to the nature and properties of sacraments, (d) it is called the body of Christ Jesus.

(a) Matt. 26: 29. (b) Eph. 5: 26; Tit. 3: 5. (c) Mark 14: 24; 1 Cor. 10: 16,17,26-28. (d) Gen. 17: 10,11,14,19; Exod. 12: 11,13,27,43,48; Exod. 13: 9; 1 Pet. 3: 21; 1 Cor. 10: 1-4.

Question 79: Why then doth Christ call the bread "his body", and the cup "his blood", or "the new covenant in his blood"; and Paul the "communion of body and blood of Christ"?

Answer: Christ speaks thus, not without great reason, namely, not only thereby to teach us, that as bread and wine support this temporal life, so his crucified body and shed blood are the true meat and drink, whereby our souls are fed to eternal life; (a) but more especially by these visible signs and pledges to assure us, that we are as really partakers of his true body and blood by the operation of the Holy Ghost as we receive by the mouths of our bodies these holy signs in remembrance of him; (b) and that all his sufferings and obedience are as certainly ours, as if we had in our own persons suffered and made satisfaction for our sins to God.

(a) John 6: 51,55. (b) 1 Cor. 10: 16,17.

Most merciful Father, we render to thee all praise, thanks, and glory, for that it hath pleased thee, of thy great mercies, to grant unto us, miserable sinners, so excellent a gift and treasure, as to receive us into the fellowship and company of thy dear Son JESUS CHRIST our Lord, whom thou hast delivered to death for us, and hast given him unto us as a necessary food and nourishment unto everlasting life.

And now, we beseech thee also, O heavenly Father, to grant us this request, that thou never suffer us to become so unkind as to forget so worthy benefits; but rather imprint and fasten them sure in our hearts, that we may grow and increase daily more and more in true faith, which continually is exercised in all manner of good works; and so much the rather, O LORD, confirm us in these perilous days and rages of Satan, that we may constantly stand and continue in the confession of the same, to the advancement of thy glory, who art GOD over all things, blessed forever. So be it. Amen. (Prayer by John Knox)

DAY 30: A MEANS OF GRACE

Question 80: What difference is there between the Lord's supper and the popish mass?

Answer: The Lord's supper testifies to us, that we have a full pardon of all sin by the only sacrifice of Jesus Christ, which he himself has once accomplished on the cross; (a) and, that we by the Holy Ghost are ingrafted into Christ, (b) who, according to his human nature is now not on earth, but in heaven, at the right hand of God his Father, (c) and will there be worshipped by us. (d) But the mass teaches, that the living and dead have not the pardon of sins through the sufferings of Christ, unless Christ is also daily offered for them by the priests; and further, that Christ is bodily under the form of bread and wine, and therefore is to be worshipped in them; so that the mass, at bottom, is nothing else than a denial of the one sacrifice and sufferings of Jesus Christ, and an accursed idolatry. (e)

(a) Heb. 7: 27; Heb. 9: 12,25-28; Heb. 10: 10,12-14; John 19: 30; Matt. 26: 28; Luke 22: 19,20. (b) 1 Cor. 6: 17; 1 Cor. 10: 16. (c) Heb. 1: 3; Heb. 8: 1,2; John 20: 17. (d) Matt. 6: 20,21; John 4: 21-24; Luke

24: 52; Acts 7: 55,56; Col. 3: 1; Philip. 3: 20,21; 1 Thess. 1: 10; Heb. 9: 6-10. (e) Heb. 9: 26; Heb. 10: 12,14,19-31.

Question 81: For whom is the Lord's supper instituted?

Answer: For those who are truly sorrowful for their sins, and yet trust that these are forgiven them for the sake of Christ; and that their remaining infirmities are covered by his passion and death; and who also earnestly desire to have their faith more and more strengthened, and their lives more holy; but hypocrites, and such as turn not to God with sincere hearts, eat and drink judgment to themselves. (a)

(a) 1 Cor. 10: 19-22; 1 Cor. 11: 28,29.

Question 82: Are they also to be admitted to this supper, who, by confession and life, declare themselves unbelieving and ungodly?

Answer: No; for by this, the covenant of God would be profaned, and his wrath kindled against the whole congregation; (a) therefore it is the duty of the Christian church, according to the appointment of Christ and his apostles, to exclude such persons, by the keys of the kingdom of heaven, till they show amendment of life.

(a) 1 Cor. 11: 20,34; Isa. 1: 11-15; Isa. 66: 3; Jer. 7: 21-23; Ps. 50: 16.

Faithful Father and Lord Jesus Christ, we know that this supper is only for those who are truly sorrowful for their sins. Make us repentant, make us willing in the day of your power. Remind us to trust that our sins are forgiven us for the sake of Christ and that our daily sins and remaining infirmities are also covered by His passion and death. Enable us, make us want to earnestly desire to have our faith more and more strengthened, our lives more holy, turning our hearts away from sin unto God so that we, with sincere hearts may eat and drink without fear of judgment. And we join in prayer with Jean Calvin when he said,

"Grant, Almighty God, that as thou dost so kindly call on us daily by thy voice, meekly and calmly to offer ourselves to be ruled by thee, and since thou hast exalted us to a high degree of honour by freeing us from the dread of the devil, and from that tyranny which kept us in miserable fear, and hast also favoured us with the Spirit of adoption and of hope, - O grant, that we, being mindful of these benefits, may ever submit ourselves to thee, and desire only to raise our voice for this end, that the whole world may submit itself to thee, and that those who seem now to rage against thee may at length be brought, as well as we, to render thee obedience, so that thy Son Christ may be the Lord of all, to the end that thou alone mayest be exalted, and that we may be made subject to thee, and be at length raised up above, and become partakers of that glory which has been obtained for us by Christ our Lord. Amen." (Calvin Commentary on Hosea).

DAY 31: KEYS OF KINGDOM OF HEAVEN

Question 83: What are the keys of the kingdom of heaven?

Answer: The preaching of the holy gospel, and Christian discipline, or excommunication out of the Christian church; by these two, the kingdom of heaven is opened to believers, and shut against unbelievers. Question 84: How is the kingdom of heaven opened and shut by the preaching of the holy gospel? Answer: Thus: when according to the command of Christ, it is declared and publicly testified to all and every believer, that, whenever they receive the promise of the gospel by a true faith, all their sins are really forgiven them of God, for the sake of Christ's merits; and on the contrary, when it is declared and testified to all unbelievers, and such as do not sincerely repent, that they stand exposed to the wrath of God, and eternal condemnation, so long as they are unconverted: (a) according to which testimony of the gospel, God will judge them, both in this, and in the life to come.

Question 85: How is the kingdom of heaven shut and opened by Christian discipline?

Answer: Thus: when according to the command of Christ, those, who under the name of Christians, maintain doctrines, or practices inconsistent therewith, and will not, after having been often brotherly admonished, renounce their errors and wicked course of life, are complained of to the church, or to those, who are thereunto appointed by the church; and if they despise their admonition, are by them forbidden the use of the sacraments; whereby they are excluded from the Christian church, and by God himself from the kingdom of Christ; and when they promise and show real amendment, are again received as members of Christ and his church. (a)

(a) Matt. 16: 18,19; Matt. 18: 15-19; John 20: 21-23.

Holy and Righteous Lord,

According to the command of Christ, we are to maintain fidelity to the doctrines of Your Church, and maintain consistent practice in the same. Grant that truth will reign in your Church, that no doctrine of the devil will be established and that those who have not maintained fidelity be brought to the truth and to repentance. Guard our hearts against vain things, strange fire and heretical teaching. By Your Spirit, keep Your Church faithful to Your Word, broadcasting the Gospel to all, especially those of the household of faith. May we, by the admonition of our pastors, whom you have given to the Church as gifts, who shepherd our souls watching out that we may neither injure ourselves or others, maintain faithfulness to the teachings Your Word has brought us. May we, by the right use of your sacraments, be fed by this holy food. Keep us from sins, from egregious public sins and forgive us even our secret sins that we dare not expose to others but lay open before You. Forgive us our trespasses and open to correction and reproof so that we may be workmen who rightly divide the Word of Truth. In Christ our Lord, Amen.

DAY 32: THANKFULNESS

Question 86: Since then we are delivered from our misery, merely of grace, through Christ, without any merit of ours, why must we still do good works?

(a) Rom. 6: 13; Rom. 12: 1,2; 1 Pet. 2: 5,9,10; 1 Cor. 6: 20. (b) Matt. 5: 16; 1 Pet. 2: 12; 1 Pet. 1: 6,7. (c) 2 Pet. 1: 10; Matt. 7: 17; Gal. 5: 6,22,23. (d) 1 Pet. 3: 1,2; Rom. 14: 19.

Answer: Because Christ, having redeemed and delivered us by his blood, also renews us by his Holy Spirit, after his own image; that so we may testify, by the whole of our conduct, our gratitude to God for his blessings, (a) and that he may be praised by us; (b) also, that every one may be assured in himself of his faith, (c) by the fruits thereof; and that, by our godly conversation others may be gained to Christ. (d)

Question 87: Cannot they then be saved, who, continuing in their wicked and ungrateful lives, are not converted to God?

Answer: By no means; for the holy scripture declares that no unchaste person, idolater, adulterer, thief, covetous man, drunkard, slanderer, robber, or any such like, shall inherit the kingdom of God.

(a)

(a) 1 Cor. 6: 9,10; Eph. 5: 5,6; 1 John 3: 14.

THE LORD is in his holy temple: let all the earth keep silence before him. Hab. ii. 20.

I was glad when they said unto me, We will go into the house of the LORD. Psalm cxxii. 1.

Let the words of my mouth, and the meditation of my heart, be alway acceptable in thy sight, O LORD, my strength and my redeemer. Psalm xix. 14.

O send out thy light and thy truth, that they may lead me, and bring me unto thy holy hill, and to thy dwelling. Psalm xliii. 3.

Thus saith the high and lofty One that inhabiteth eternity, whose name is Holy; I dwell in the high and holy place, with him also that is of a contrite and humble spirit, to revive the spirit of the humble, and to revive the heart of the contrite ones. Isaiah lvii. 15.

The hour cometh, and now is, when the true worshippers shall worship the Father in spirit and in truth: for the Father seeketh such to worship him. St. John iv. 23.

Grace be unto you, and peace, from God our Father, and from the Lord Jesus Christ. Phil. i. 2. *(Book of Common Prayer)*

DAY 33: TRUE CONVERSION

Question 88: Of how many parts does the true conversion of man consist?

Answer: Of two parts; of the mortification of the old, and the quickening of the new man. (a)

(a) *Rom. 6: 1,4-6; Eph. 4: 22-24; Col. 3: 5-10; 1 Cor. 5: 7; 2 Cor. 7: 10.*

Question 89: What is the mortification of the old man?

Answer: It is a sincere sorrow of heart, that we have provoked God by our sins; and more and more to hate and flee from them. (a)

(a) *Rom. 8: 13; Joel 2: 13; Hos. 6: 1.*

Question 90: What is the quickening of the new man?

Answer: It is a sincere joy of heart in God, through Christ, (a) and with love and delight to live according to the will of God in all good works. (b)

(a) *Rom. 5: 1; Rom. 14: 17; Isa. 57: 15. (b) Rom. 6: 10,11; Gal. 2: 20.*

Question 91: But what are good works?

Answer: Only those which proceed from a true faith, (a) are performed according to the law of God, (b) and to his glory; (c) and not such as are founded on our imaginations, or the institutions of men. (d)

(a) *Rom. 14: 23. (b) Lev. 18: 4; 1 Sam. 15: 22; Eph. 2: 10. (c) 1 Cor. 10: 31. (d) Deut. 12: 32; Ezek. 20: 18,19; Isa. 29: 13; Matt. 15: 7-9.*

Merciful Father, only two parts reveal true conversion; the mortification of the old man and the quickening of the new. Though we know our old man is crucified with Christ, yet too often we give up our members unto uncleanness, covetousness, and a myriad of other sins, all of which are abhorrent in your site. Give us a sincere sorrow of heart that we might be provoked by Your Holy Spirit for ours sins and help us to more and more hate and flee from them. Enable us to live after the Spirit, through Whom we mortify the deeds of the body. Teach us to rend our hearts and not our garments, to turn to You when we sin, for You, LORD God, are gracious and merciful, slow to anger, and of great kindness, and though you may smight us for a season, you will bind us up.

Grant unto us a sincere joy of heart in You, through Christ so that with love and delight we might live according to Your Most Holy Will, which we read of in the Scriptures and unto all good works. We know that our works will never justify us for you have justified us by grace through faith. Only those good works which proceed from a true faith, are done according to your Law and for your glory alone are acceptable to you. Our own vain imaginations as what pleases you, nor the institutions of man, will ever be received, so equip us by Your Spirit to live Coram Deo, before Your face always. Amen.

DAY 34: THE LAW OF GOD

Question 92: What is the law of God?

Answer: God spake all these words, Exodus 20:1-17 and Denteronomy 5:6-21, saying: I am the LORD thy God, which have brought thee out of the land of Egypt, out of the house of bondage.

1st commandment: Thou shalt have no other gods before me.

2nd commandment: Thou shalt not make unto thee any graven image, or any likeness of any thing that is in heaven above, or that is in the earth beneath, or that is in the water under the earth. Thou shalt not bow down thyself to them, nor serve them; for I the LORD thy God am a jealous God, visiting the iniquity of the fathers upon the children unto the third and fourth generation of them that hate me, and shewing mercy unto thousands of them that love me, and keep my commandments.

3rd commandment: Thou shalt not take the name of the LORD thy God in vain; for the LORD will not hold him guiltless that taketh his name in vain.

4th commandment: Remember the sabbath day, to keep it holy. Six days shalt thou labour, and do all thy work; but the seventh day is the sabbath of the LORD thy God: in it thou shalt not do any work, thou, nor thy son, nor thy daughter, thy manservant, nor thy maidservant, nor thy cattle, nor thy stranger that is within thy gates. For in six days the LORD made heaven and earth, the sea, and all that in them is, and rested the seventh day: wherefore the LORD blessed the sabbath day, and hallowed it.

5th commandment: Honour thy father and thy mother: that thy days may be long upon the land which the LORD thy God giveth thee.

6th commandment: Thou shalt not kill.

7th commandment: Thou shalt not commit adultery.

8th commandment: Thou shalt not steal.

9th commandment: Thou shalt not bear false witness against thy neighbour.

10th commandment: Thou shalt not covet thy neighbour's house, thou shalt not covet thy neighbour's wife, nor his manservant, nor his maidservant, nor his ox, nor his ass, nor any thing that is thy neighbour's.

Question 93: How are these commandments divided?

Answer: Into two tables; (a) the first of which teaches us how we must behave towards God; the second, what duties we owe to our neighbour. (b)

(a) Exod. 34: 28; Deut. 4: 13; Deut. 10: 3,4. (b) Matt. 22: 37-40.

Question 94: What does God enjoin in the first commandment?

Answer: That I, as sincerely as I desire the salvation of my own soul, avoid and flee from all idolatry, (a) sorcery, soothsaying, superstition, (b) invocation of saints, or any other creatures; (c) and learn rightly to know the only true God; (d) trust in him alone, (e) with humility (f) and patience submit to him; (g) expect all good things from him only; (h) love, (i) fear, (j) and glorify him with my whole heart; (k) so that I renounce and forsake all creatures, rather than commit even the least thing contrary to his will. (l)

(a) 1 John 5 :21; 1 Cor. 6: 9,10; 1 Cor. 10: 7,14. (b) Lev. 19: 31; Deut. 18: 9- 12. (c) Matt. 4: 10; Rev. 19: 10; Rev. 22: 8,9. (d) John 17: 3. (e) Jer. 17: 5,7. (f) 1 Pet. 5: 5,6. (g) Heb. 10: 36; Col. 1: 11; Rom. 5: 3,4; 1 Cor. 10: 10; Philip. 2: 14. (h) Ps. 104: 27-30; Isa. 45: 7; James 1: 17. (i) Deut. 6: 5; Matt. 22: 37. (j) Deut. 6: 2; Ps. 111: 10; Prov. 1: 7; Prov. 9: 10; Matt. 10: 28. (k) Matt. 4: 10; Deut. 10: 20,21. (l) Matt. 5: 29,30; Matt. 10: 37; Acts 5: 29.

Question 95: What is idolatry?

Answer: Idolatry is, instead of, or besides that one true God, who has manifested himself in his word, to contrive, or have any other object, in which men place their trust. (a)

(a) Eph. 5: 5; 1 Chron. 16: 26; Philip. 3: 19; Gal. 4: 8; Eph. 2: 12; 1 John 2: 23; 2 John 1: 9; John 5: 23.

Holy, Holy Holy, LORD God Almighty, You have given us your Commandments and we have rejected them, spat upon them, denied them, rebuked them and cast them aside because we are sinners. In Your first command you call us to desire the salvation of our own souls, avoid and flee from all idolatry, sorcery, soothsaying, superstition, invocation of saints, or any other creature. Yet, we have not done this. You call us to rightly know the One and Only True and Living God, to trust in You alone, with humility and patience submitting to you, expecting all good things from You alone, but we have looked to others instead. You have called us to love, fear and glorify you with all our heart, soul and mind, and we have sinned grievously in our rejection of you. Teach us to renounce and forsake all other creatures, and rather help us to commit to You alone, rejecting even the least thing which is contrary to your will.

We have been idolatrous because we have magnified others above the One True God, though you have manifest yourself in the Word. Teach us to trust no other object but rely completely upon You, through the Power of Your Holy Spirit by the Name of Jesus we implore you to come to our aid for we are weak, we are sinners and we are lost without You. Amen.

DAY 35: REJECTION OF IMAGES OF GOD

Question 96: *What does God require in the second commandment?*

Answer: That we in no wise represent God by images, (a) nor worship him in any other way than he has commanded in his word. (b)

(a) Deut. 4: 15-19; Isa. 40: 18-25; Rom. 1: 23,24; Acts 17: 29. (b) 1 Sam. 15: 23; Deut. 12: 30-32; Matt. 15: 9.

Question 97: *Are images then not at all to be made?*

Answer: God neither can, nor may be represented by any means: (a) but as to creatures; though they may be represented, yet God forbids to make, or have any resemblance of them, either in order to worship them or to serve God by them. (b)

(a) Isa. 40: 25. (b) Exod. 23: 24,25; Exod. 34: 13,14,17; Num. 33: 52; Deut. 7: 5; Deut. 12: 3; Deut. 16: 21; 2 Kin. 18: 3,4.

Question 98: But may not images be tolerated in the churches, as books to the laity?

Answer: No: for we must not pretend to be wiser than God, who will have his people taught, not by dumb images, (a) but by the lively preaching of his word. (b)

(a) Jer. 10: 8; Hab. 2: 18,19. (b) Rom. 10: 14,15,17; 2 Pet. 1: 19; 2 Tim. 3: 16,17.

Almighty and Everlasting God, You alone are God and apart from Thee there is no other. Help us to know that no image can ever give us a true picture of Who You are, and in fact, so detract from your Glory as to be loathsome and offensive to You. Teach us that we are to worship you only in the way that You have commanded us by Your Word. Remind us that even pictures of Jesus are forbidden as He is God the Son, Blessed Holy Spirit and the same for the Blessed Third Person of the Holy Trinity, The Holy Spirit. Keep us ever vigilant to keep far from idols or any resemblance of You either in worship or in ways that feeble man thinks as helps to worship. We are not wiser than You, who will have Your people taught, not by dumb images but by the lively preaching of Your Word. Amen.

DAY 36: RIGHT WORSHIP

Question 99: What is required in the third commandment?

Answer: That we, not only by cursing (a) or perjury, (b) but also by rash swearing, (c) must not profane or abuse the name of God; nor by silence or connivance be partakers of these horrible sins in others; (d) and, briefly, that we use the holy name of God no otherwise than with fear and reverence; (e) so that he may be rightly confessed (f) and worshipped by us, (g) and be glorified in all our words and works. (h)

(a) Lev. 24: 11-16. (b) Lev. 19: 12. (c) Matt. 5: 37; James 5: 12. (d) Lev. 5: 1; Prov. 29: 24. (e) Jer. 4: 2; Isa. 45: 23. (f) Rom. 10: 9,10; Matt. 10: 32. (g) Ps. 50: 15; 1 Tim. 2: 8. (h) Rom. 2: 24; 1 Tim. 6: 1; Col. 3: 16,17.

Question 100: Is then the profaning of God's name, by swearing and cursing, so heinous a sin, that his wrath is kindled against those who do not endeavour, as much as in them lies, to prevent and forbid such cursing and swearing?

Answer: It undoubtedly is, (a) for there is no sin greater or more provoking to God, than the profaning of his name; and therefore he has commanded this sin to be punished with death. (b)

(a) Prov. 29: 24; Lev. 5: 1. (b) Lev. 24: 15,16.

Holy Father,

Too often we are quick with our words and the result is that we curse or perjury ourselves. We speak too rashly and swear or profane and abuse the Name of God. Often, in our silence, we become partakers of these horrible sins in others and forget that we should stand for His Nam before the world. Many times we come to worship without fear and reverence and then take the glory unto ourselves. Keep us vigilant in preserving the honor and integrity of Your Most Holy Name. Amen.

DAY 37: KEEP HIS NAME HOLY

Question 101: May we then swear religiously by the name of God?

Answer: Yes: either when the magistrates demand it of the subjects; or when necessity requires us thereby to confirm a fidelity and truth to the glory of God, and the safety of our neighbour: for such an oath is founded on God's word, (a) and therefore was justly used by the saints, both in the Old and New Testament. (b)

(a) Deut. 6: 13; Deut. 10: 20; Isa. 48: 1; Heb. 6: 16. (b) Gen. 21: 24; Gen. 31: 53,54; Jos. 9: 15,19 ; 1 Sam. 24: 22; 2 Sam. 3: 35; 1 Kin. 1: 28-30; Rom. 1: 9; 2 Cor. 1: 23.

Question 102: May we also swear by saints or any other creatures?

Answer: No; for a lawful oath is calling upon God, as the only one who knows the heart, that he will bear witness to the truth, and punish me if I swear falsely; (a) which honour is due to no creature. (b)

(a) 2 Cor. 1: 23; Rom. 9: 1. (b) Matt. 5: 34-36; James 5: 12.

Most Gracious Judge and Heavenly Father, Teach us to discern when it is of necessity to confirm a fidelity and truth to the Glory of Your Name, so that the safety of our neighbor is preserved for such an oath is founded upon Your Word. May we never take a lawful oath upon another other name here, but remember You alone are the only one who knows the heart and You will bear witness to all truth and punish us if we swear falsely. May we, in all our words, bring honor to Your Name alone.

DAY 38: KEEP THE SABBATH

Question 103: What does God require in the fourth commandment?

Answer: First, that the ministry of the gospel and the schools be maintained; (a) and that I, especially on the sabbath, that is, on the day of rest, diligently frequent the church of God, (b) to hear his word, (c) to use the sacraments, (d) publicly to call upon the Lord, (e) and contribute to the relief of the poor. (f) Secondly, that all the days of my life I cease from my evil works, and yield myself to the Lord, to work by his Holy Spirit in me: and thus begin in this life the eternal sabbath. (g)

(a) Tit. 1: 5; 2 Tim. 3: 14,15; 1 Tim. 5: 17; 1 Cor. 9: 11,13,14; 2 Tim. 2: 2. (b) Ps. 40: 10,11; Ps. 68: 27; Acts 2: 42,46. (c) 1 Tim. 4: 13,19; 1 Cor. 14: 29,31. (d) 1 Cor. 11: 33. (e) 1 Tim .2: 1-3,8-11; 1 Cor. 14: 16. (f) 1 Cor. 16: 2. (g) Isa. 66: 23.

Lord God, Creator of All, After You had created all things by the Word of Your Power, spoken into being not evolved, created ex nihilo (out of nothing), on that Seventh Day You rested. We read your command here to keep the Sabbath holy, and yet forget that You have good reason for us to rest as well, as a foretaste of that Eternal Rest we, your people, all long for. Teach us that the First Day of the Week, the day of the New Creation, the Day Jesus our Savior rose from the dead, having satisfied Your Law on behalf of His People, that it is a celebration of the victory over the grave and a reminder that we are the New Creation created in Christ Jesus unto good works. Teach us that on this First Day of the week, Your gospel is to be taught in the congregation of the holy and in all schools. Grant us ears to hear Your Word, to be fed by Your sacraments, to publically call upon the Lord and contribute to the relief of the poor.

On this day of rest, remind us that all the days of our lives we are to cease from our evil works and yield ourselves up to God to work by His Holy Spirit and thus begin in this life the eternal Sabbath. Amen.

DAY 39: HONOR THOSE IN AUTHORITY

Question 104: What does God require in the fifth commandment?

Answer: That I show all honour, love and fidelity, to my father and mother, and all in authority over me, and submit myself to their good instruction and correction, with due obedience; (a) and also patiently bear with their weaknesses and infirmities, (b) since it pleases God to govern us by their hand. (c)

(a) Eph. 5: 22; Eph. 6: 1-5; Col. 3: 18,20-24; Prov. 1: 8; Prov. 4: 1; Prov. 15: 20; Prov. 20: 20; Exod. 21: 17; Rom. 13: 1-7. (b) Prov. 23: 22; Gen. 9: 24,25; 1 Pet. 2: 18. (c) Eph. 6: 4,9; Col .3: 19-21; Rom. 13: 2,3; Matt. 22: 21.

Lord God, Master and Savior,

First, teach us to honor, love, show fidelity to You, our Faithful Father in Heaven. May we show that love and honor to our earthly parents and all in authority over us. By Your Spirit, teach us to submit ourselves to their good instruction and correction, with due obedience. When they are frail, help us to patiently love and serve them. You have placed others over us to watch for our souls. Grant them the necessary grace to serve us, protect and teach us all things from Your Word. Make us willing servants to those in authority over us so that the Name of Christ suffers no injustice or shame and may we, this day, serve others so that You may receive Glory and they may glory in you too. Amen.

DAY 40:

Question 105: What does God require in the sixth commandment?

Answer: That neither in thoughts, nor words, nor gestures, much less in deeds, I dishonour, hate, wound, or kill my neighbour, by myself or by another: (a) but that I lay aside all desire of revenge: (b) also, that I hurt not myself, nor wilfully expose myself to any danger. (c) Wherefore also the magistrate is armed with the sword, to prevent murder. (d)

(a) Matt. 5: 21,22; Matt. 26: 52; Gen. 9: 6. (b) Eph. 4: 26; Rom. 12: 19; Matt. 5: 25; Matt. 18: 35. (c) Rom. 13: 14; Col. 2: 23; Matt. 4: 7. (d) Gen. 9: 6; Exod. 21: 14; Matt. 26: 52; Rom. 13: 4.

Question 106: But this commandment seems only to speak of murder?

Answer: In forbidding murder, God teaches us, that he abhors the causes thereof, such as envy, (a) hatred, (b) anger, (c) and desire of revenge; and that he accounts all these as murder. (d)

(a) Prov. 14: 30; Rom. 1: 29. (b) 1 John 2: 9,11. (c) James 1: 20; Gal. 5: 19,21. (d) 1 John 3: 15.

Question 107: But is it enough that we do not kill any man in the manner mentioned above?

Answer: No: for when God forbids envy, hatred, and anger, he commands us to love our neighbour as ourselves; (a) to show patience, peace, meekness, mercy, and all kindness, towards him, (b) and prevent his hurt as much as in us lies; (c) and that we do good, even to our enemies. (d)

(a) Matt. 7: 12; Matt. 22: 39; Rom. 12: 10. (b) Eph. 4: 2; Gal. 6: 1,2; Matt. 5: 5,7,9; Rom. 12: 18; Luke 6: 36; 1 Pet. 3: 8; Col. 3: 12; Rom. 12: 10,15. (c) Exod. 23: 5. (d) Matt. 5: 44,45; Rom. 12: 20,21.

Gracious God and Lord our Savior, So often in thought, word, gestures and deed we dishonor, hate, wound, kill our neighbor, either ourselves or by another. Teach us to lay aside all revenge, that we will not hurt ourselves nor willfully expose ourselves to danger. We pray that you would enable those in authority over us in the government to protect the lives of others as well. Yet, we know that physical murder and harm are not the full extent to which we are to protect all life, but you teach us that envy, hatred, anger, and desire of revenge, all these are equal to murder in Your eyes. You forbid these actions and intents of the heart and are instead to show patience, peace, meekness, mercy and all kindness towards others, even our enemies, for so did Christ on that night He was betrayed. Though He could have called a legion of angels, he chose to be mocked, whipped, spat upon and cursed, rather than to charge after those who sought His life. Make us meek like Christ and give us understanding at those times too. Help us to prevent the hurt of our enemies, as much as lies in us, that we will do good even to our enemy as well as the enemies of the Cross of Christ and His Kingdom. Amen.

DAY 41: KEEPING OURSELVES PURE UNTO MARRIAGE

Question 108: What does the seventh commandment teach us?

Answer: That all uncleanness is accursed of God: (a) and that therefore we must with all our hearts detest the same, (b) and live chastely and temperately, (c) whether in holy wedlock, or in single life. (d)

(a) Lev. 18: 27,28. (b) Jude 1: 23. (c) 1 Thess. 4: 3-5. (d) Heb. 13: 4; 1 Cor. 7: 7-9,27.

Question 109: Does God forbid in this commandment, only adultery, and such like gross sins?

Answer: Since both our body and soul are temples of the holy Ghost, he commands us to preserve them pure and holy: therefore he forbids all unchaste actions, gestures, words, (a) thoughts, desires, (b) and whatever can entice men thereto. (c)

(a) Eph. 5: 3,4; 1 Cor. 6: 18-20. (b) Matt. 5: 27,28. (c) Eph. 5: 18; 1 Cor. 15: 33.

Holy Father, In this vile and sinful world, it is so easy for our eyes to see filth and uncleanness. It is so hard to remain chaste and live temperately in the muck and mire of the world. However, both our body and soul are temples of Your Holy Spirit and you command us to persevere them pure and holy, therefore, keep us from all temptation to unchaste actions, gestures, words, thoughts, desires and whatever can entice us thereto. Through Christ our Lord we pray, Amen.

DAY 42: THOU SHALT NOT STEAL

Question 110: What does God forbid in the eighth commandment?

Answer: God forbids not only those thefts, (a) and robberies, (b) which are punishable by the magistrate; but he comprehends under the name of theft all wicked tricks and devices, whereby we design to appropriate to ourselves the goods which belong to our neighbour: (c) whether it be by force, or under the appearance of right, as by unjust weights, ells, measures, fraudulent merchandise, (d) false coins, usury, (e) or by any other way forbidden by God; as also all covetousness, (f) all abuse and waste of his gifts. (g)

(a) 1 Cor. 6: 10. (b) 1 Cor. 5: 10; Isa. 33: 1. (c) Luke 3: 14; 1 Thess. 4: 6. (d) Prov. 11: 1; Prov. 16: 11; Ezek. 45: 9-12; Deut. 25: 13-16. (e) Ps. 15: 5; Luke 6: 35. (f) 1 Cor. 6: 10. (g) Prov. 23: 20,21; Prov. 21: 20.

Question 111: But what does God require in this commandment?

Answer: That I promote the advantage of my neighbour in every instance I can or may; and deal with him as I desire to be dealt with by others: (a) further also that I faithfully labour, so that I may be able to relieve the needy. (b)

(a) Matt. 7: 12. (b) Eph. 4: 28.

Lord God, Holy is Your Name. You are the God who supplies for our every need. How could we not rely upon you and therefore, steal, to satisfy our wants and desires. Forgive us for not trusting You to supply for our every need, in and through Christ Jesus our Lord and Savior. We repent that we have tried by tricks and devices to defraud our fellow man and through covetousness have brought about the schemes of the devil by our own hands. Teach us that You supply all things to promote the advantage of our neighbors in every instance. Show us that we own nothing; that we were born naked and naked we return to dust. Help us to aid our fellow man, to treat him with the same love we would want to be treated with, and that we may faithfully labor, so that we can relieve the needy. Amen.

DAY 43: SPEAK THE TRUTH

Question 112: What is required in the ninth commandment?

Answer: That I bear false witness against no man, (a) nor falsify any man's words; (b) that I be no backbiter, nor slanderer; (c) that I do not judge, nor join in condemning any man rashly, or unheard; (d) but that I avoid all sorts of lies and deceit, as the proper works of the devil, (e) unless I would bring down upon me the heavy wrath of God; (f) likewise, that in judgment and all other dealings I love the truth, speak it uprightly and confess it; (g) also that I defend and promote, as much as I am able, the honor and good character of my neighbour. (h)

(a) Prov. 19: 5,9; Prov. 21: 28. (b) Ps. 15: 3; Ps. 50: 19,20. (c) Rom. 1: 29,30. (d) Matt. 7: 1,2; Luke 6: 37. (e) John 8: 44. (f) Prov. 12: 22; Prov. 13: 5. (g) 1 Cor. 13: 6; Eph. 4: 25. (h) 1 Pet. 4: 8.

Lord God, You desire truth in the inward parts. Jesus declared that He is the Way, the TRUTH and the life. Grant that we will not bear false witness against no man, nor falsify any man's words; that we be no backbiter, nor slanderer of our fellow man. Too often we judge rashly and not rightly, condemning them though we have not heard nor seen what they have done. Teach us that our tongue is a powerful member, like the rudder of a great ship, much harm comes from our lips when we deceive. Help to avoid all sorts of lies and deceit for it is the devil whom You call the "father of lies" and we, though once we were, are not now sons and daughters of darkness, but have been translated in the Kingdom of Light. Remind us that when we lie the heavy judgment of God will bring us down. May we deal only in truth, may we love truth, speak it uprightly and confess it, may we defend and promote, as much as we are able, the honor and good character of our neighbors, through Christ our Lord we ask, Amen.

DAY 44: BEING CONTENT IN ALL THINGS

Question 113: What does the tenth commandment require of us?

Answer: That even the smallest inclination or thought, contrary to any of God's commandments, never rise in our hearts; but that at all times we hate all sin with our whole heart, and delight in all righteousness. (a)

(a) Rom. 7: (a) Rom. 7: 7.

Question 114: But can those who are converted to God perfectly keep these commandments?

Answer: No: but even the holiest men, while in this life, have only a small beginning of this obedience; (a) yet so, that with a sincere resolution they begin to live, not only according to some, but all the commandments of God. (b)

(a) 1 John 1: 8-10; Rom. 7: 14,15; Eccl. 7: 20; 1 Cor. 13: 9. (b) Rom. 7: 22; Ps. 1: 2; James 2: 10.

Question 115: Why will God then have the ten commandments so strictly preached, since no man in this life can keep them?

Answer: First, that all our lifetime we may learn more and more to know (a) our sinful nature, and thus become the more earnest in seeking the remission of sin, and righteousness in Christ; (b) likewise, that we constantly endeavour and pray to God for the grace of the Holy Spirit, that we may become more and more conformable to the image of God, till we arrive at the perfection proposed to us, in a life to come. (c)

(a) Rom. 3: 20; 1 John 1: 9; Ps. 32: 5. (b) Matt. 5: 6; Rom. 7: 24,25. (c) 1 Cor. 9: 24; Philip. 3: 11-14.

Lord God Almighty,

As the Apostle Paul said, had he not seen "thou shalt not covet" he would not have known his sin. So too, we have desired that which is not our own, which You have not seen in Your wisdom to give us. Like spoiled children we thrash about in our minds and hearts demanding You to give us what we want even if it belongs to another. Oh, may even the smallest inclination or thought, contrary to any of your Commandments, never rise in our heats, but that at all times we hate all sin with our whole heart and delight in righteousness alone.

Remind us that while in this life we have only a small beginning of this obedience and give us a sincere resolution to begin to live, not only according to some, but to all the commands of God. Lord, may we make our life a time that we learn more and more to know our sinful nature and thus become the more earnest in seeking the remission of all our sins, finding comfort in the Righteousness of Christ alone.

Likewise, by the power of Your Holy Spirit, your grace would be what we constantly endeavored and asked from you that mercy to receive, so that we may become more and more conformable to the image of God, until we arrive at the perfection proposed to us in the life to come. Amen.

DAY 45: NECESSITY OF PRAYER

Question 116: Why is prayer necessary for Christians?

Answer: Because it is the chief part of thankfulness which God requires of us: (a) and also, because God will give his grace and Holy Spirit to those only, who with sincere desires continually ask them of him, and are thankful for them. (b)

(a) Ps. 50: 14,15. (b) Matt. 7: 7,8; Luke 11: 9,10,13; 1 Thess. 5: 17.

Question 117: What are the requisites of that prayer, which is acceptable to God, and which he will hear?

Answer: First, that we from the heart pray (a) to the one true God only, who has manifested himself in his word, (b) for all things, he has commanded us to ask of him; (c) secondly, that we rightly and thoroughly know our need and misery, (d) that so we may deeply humble ourselves in the presence of his divine majesty; (e) thirdly, that we be fully persuaded that he, notwithstanding that we are unworthy of it, will, for the sake of Christ our Lord, certainly hear our prayer, (f) as he has promised us in his word. (g)

(a) John 4: 24; Ps. 145: 18. (b) Rev. 19: 10; John 4: 22-24. (c) Rom.

8: 26; 1 John 5: 14; James 1: 5. (d) 2 Chron. 20: 12. (e) Ps. 2: 11; Ps. 34: 19; Isa. 66: 2. (f) Rom. 10: 14; James 1: 6. (g) John 14: 13,14; John 16: 23; Dan. 9: 17,18. (h) Matt. 7: 8; Ps. 27: 8.

Question 118: What has God commanded us to ask of him?

Answer: All things necessary for soul and body; (a) which Christ our Lord has comprised in that prayer he himself has taught us. (a) James 1:17 Every good gift and every perfect gift is from above, and cometh down from the Father of lights, with whom is no variableness, neither shadow of turning. Matthew 6:33 But seek ye first the kingdom of God, and his righteousness; and all these things shall be added unto you.

(a)   James 1: 17; Matt. 6: 33.

Question 119: What are the words of that prayer? (a)

Answer: Our Father which art in heaven, 1 Hallowed be thy name. 2 Thy kingdom come. 3 Thy will be done on earth, as it is in heaven. 4 Give us this day our daily bread. 5 And forgive us our debts, as we forgive our debtors. 6 And lead us not into temptation, but deliver us from evil. For thine is the kingdom, and the power, and the glory, for ever. Amen.

(a) Matt. 6: 9-13; Luke 11: 2-4.

Lord God and Father of our Lord Jesus Christ, Lord, when you were here your disciples asked "Lord, teach us to pray." That is our prayer today. Help us, your people, pray so that we will show we are thankful and also that You will give Your grace the Holy Spirit to those who with sincere desire continually ask them of You and are thankful for them. We offer unto you our thanksgiving and call upon you in the day of trouble. We ask, seek, knock, knowing You hear us and will answer according to Your Eternal Will.

First, we pray from the heart to You, the One True and living God, who has manifested Yourself in Your Word, for all thing, you have commanded us to ask of You. We rightly and thoroughly know our need and misery, and so grant us the longing to humble ourselves in You're the Presence of Your Divine Majesty. We are fully persuaded that we are unworthy of any answer, but for the sake of Christ our Lord, you will certainly hear our prayer as You have promised in Your Word. And so, we ask of You all things necessary for soul and body knowing that every good gift and every perfect gift is from above, and comes down from our Father of lights, which whom is no variableness, neither shadow of turning, seeking first the kingdom of God and His righteousness being comforted that all these things shall be added unto us, through Jesus Christ our Lord who lives and reigns with both the Father and The Holy Spirit, Blessed Trinity. Amen.

DAY 46: OUR FATHER

Question 120: Why has Christ commanded us to address God thus: "Our Father"?

Answer: That immediately, in the very beginning of our prayer, he might excite in us a childlike reverence for, and confidence in God, which are the foundation of our prayer: namely, that God is become our Father in Christ, and will much less deny us what we ask of him in true faith, than our parents will refuse us earthly things. (a)

(a) Matt. 7: 9-11; Luke 11: 11-13.

Question 121: Why is it here added, "Which art in heaven"?

Answer: Lest we should form any earthly conceptions of God's heavenly majesty, (a) and that we may expect from his almighty power all things necessary for soul and body. (b)

(a) Jer. 23: 23,24; Acts 17: 24,25,27. (b) Rom. 10: 12.

Lord God, Jesus Christ, You taught us to first pray, Our Father, so that in the very beginning of our prayer we might remember that we are His Children because You have called us by Your Holy Spirit, regenerated us and adopted us. We draw near with confidence in God, and that comforts us to know that God is our Father in Christ and will much less deny us what we ask than our parents would refuse us earthly things. Lest we forget that our Father in Christ is also God of gods, Lord of lords, we remember your heavenly majesty and that we may expect from the Almighty power all things necessary for soul and body. We are comforted that neither good nor bad, rain or drought, feast or famine is from our Heavenly Father's Hand and we praise You for Your Glorious Majesty. Amen.

DAY 47: FIRST PETITION: HALLOWED BE THY NAME

Question 122: Which is the first petition?

Answer: "Hallowed be thy name"; that is, grant us, first, rightly to know thee, (a) and to sanctify, glorify and praise thee, (b) in all thy works, in which thy power, wisdom, goodness, justice, mercy and truth, are clearly displayed; and further also, that we may so order and direct our whole lives, our thoughts, words and actions, that thy name may never be blasphemed, but rather honoured and praised on our account. (c)

(a) John 17: 3; Jer. 9: 24; Jer. 31: 33,34; Matt. 16: 17; James 1: 5; Ps. 119: 105. (b) Ps. 119: 137; Luke 1: 46,47,68,69; Rom. 11: 33-36. (c) Ps. 71: 8; Ps. 115: 1.

Gracious God, Who dwells in Majesty, grant us first, to rightly know Thee, to sanctify, glorify and praise thee in all thy works, in which thy power, wisdom, goodness, justice, mercy and truth, are clearly displayed. Further, we ask that we may so order and direct our whole lives, our thoughts, words and actions, that Your Name may never be blasphemed but rather honored and praised on our account. We glory in You, that you understand and know us, that You are the LORD who exercises loving-kindness, judgment and righteousness in the earth. Teach us to Know the LORD and forgive our iniquity and remember our sins no more. Righteous are You, O LORD, and upright are your judgments, our soul magnifies the Lord and our spirit rejoice in God our Savior. You have visited and redeemed Your People and have raised up a horn of salvation for us in the house of Your servant David. O the depth of the riches both of the wisdom and knowledge of God! How unsearchable are your judgments and your ways past finding out. Who has know Your mind, O LORD or been you counselor, for it is of You and through You and to You are all things; to whom be glory now and forever more, Amen.

DAY 48: SECOND PETITION: THY KINGDOM COME

Question 123: Which is the second petition?

Answer: "Thy kingdom come"; that is, rule us so by thy word and Spirit, that we may submit ourselves more and more to thee; (a) preserve and increase thy church; (b) destroy the works of the devil, and all violence which would exalt itself against thee; and also all wicked counsels devised against thy holy word; (c) till the full perfection of thy kingdom take place, (d) wherein thou shalt be all in all. (e)

(a) Matt. 6: 33; Ps. 119: 5; Ps. 143: 10. (b) Ps. 51: 18; Ps. 122: 6-9. (c) 1 John 3: 8; Rom. 16: 20 . (d) Rev. 22: 17,20; Rom .8: 22,23. (e) 1 Cor. 15: 28.

Gracious God, Father of our Lord Jesus Christ and all whom You should call, So rule in us by your Word and Spirit that we may submit ourselves more and more to thee. O that our ways were direct to keep Your statutes! Teach us to do Your will, for You are our God; lead us into the land of uprightness. Build the walls of Jerusalem, Your People from both Jews and Gentiles, all in the same faith as father Abraham, grafted into that one tree The People of God. Preserve Thy Church and increase her; oh that those whom You have ordained unto salvation would join her today. Destroy the works of the devil and all who would do your Church harm. May there be peace within thy walls and prosperity with her palaces. Destroy the plans of the wicked counsels devised against thy Holy Word till the full perfection of thy Kingdom take place and then all shall be in all. For Christ's sake, protect your church. For Your Word says that the gates of Hell shall not prevail against her, so strengthen her, keep her from error. Disperse those with another gospel, who look to their prayers, their decisions, their works for your favor. May they see their end is destruction. Grant that today your Church will have added to Her such as should be saved that Christ may see the travail of his soul and be satisfied. Amen.

DAY 49: THIRD PETITION: THY WILL BE DONE.

Question 124: Which is the third petition?

Answer: "Thy will be done on earth as it is in heaven"; that is, grant that we and all men may renounce our own will, (a) and without murmuring obey thy will, which is only good; (b) that every one may attend to, and perform the duties of his station and calling, (c) as willingly and faithfully as the angels do in heaven. (d)

(a) Matt .16: 24; Tit. 2: 11,12. (b) Luke 22: 42; Eph. 5: 10; Rom. 12: 2. (c) 1 Cor. 7: 24. (d) Ps. 103: 20,21.

Father God, grant that we and all men may renounce3 our own will, denying ourselves and taking up His cross, teaching us that, denying ungodliness and world lusts, we should live soberly, righteously, and godly in this present world. That we would obey your will without murmuring and that everyone would attend to, and perform the duties of his station and calling, as willingly and faithfully as the angels do in heaven. Amen.

DAY 50: FOURTH PETITION: DAILY BREAD

Question 125: Which is the fourth petition?

Answer: "Give us this day our daily bread"; that is, be pleased to provide us with all things necessary for the body, (a) that we may thereby acknowledge thee to be the only fountain of all good, (b) and that neither our care nor industry, nor even thy gifts, can profit us without thy blessing; (c) and therefore that we may withdraw our trust from all creatures, and place it alone in thee. (d)

(a) Ps. 104: 27,28; Ps. 145: 15,16; Matt. 6: 25,26. (b) James 1: 17; Acts 14: 17; Acts 17: 27,28. (c) 1 Cor. 15: 58; Deut. 8: 3; Ps. 37: 3-5,16;

Gracious and Faithful Father, may we never be so rich that we forget thee, nor so poor that we steal and bring shame to Your Majestic and Holy Name. Be please to provide us with all things necessary for the body, that we may thereby acknowledge thee to be the only fountain of all good, and that neither our care nor industry, nor even they gifts, can profit us without thy blessing. Therefore, may we look away and not trust in any created thing but place it in you alone. Amen.

DAY 51: FIFTH PETITION: FORGIVENESS

Question 126: Which is the fifth petition?

Answer: "And forgive us our debts as we forgive our debtors"; that is, be pleased for the sake of Christ's blood, not to impute to us poor sinners, our transgressions, nor that depravity, which always cleaves to us; (a) even as we feel this evidence of thy grace in us, that it is our firm resolution from the heart to forgive our neighbour. (b)

(a) Ps. 51: 1-7; Ps. 143: 2; 1 John 2: 1,2; Rom. 8: 1. (b) Matt. 6: 14,15.

Have mercy upon us, O God, according to thy loving-kindness; according to the multitude of Your mercies blot out our transgressions. Daily we sin and daily we come to You, through Jesus Christ who is our Advocate, forgive us our many sins. Be pleased for the sake of Christ's blood, not to impute to us poor sinners, our transgressions, nor that depravity which always cleaves to us, but cleanse us. Even though we feel this evidence of your grace within us, that it is our firm resolution from the heart to forgive our neighbor and bring honor and glory to the Name of Christ, you Son who is the propitiation for our sins and that of the world. Amen.

DAY 52: SIXTH PETITION:
DELIVER US…AMEN.

Question 127: Which is the sixth petition?

Answer: "And lead us not into temptation, but deliver us from evil"; that is, since we are so weak in ourselves, that we cannot stand a moment; (a) and besides this, since our mortal enemies, the devil, (b) the world, (c) and our own flesh, (d) cease not to assault us, do thou therefore preserve and strengthen us by the power of thy Holy Spirit, that we may not be overcome in this spiritual warfare, (e) but constantly and strenuously may resist our foes, till at last we obtain a complete victory. (f)

(a) John 15: 5; Ps. 103: 14. (b) 1 Pet. 5: 8; Eph. 6: 12. (c) John 15: 19. (d) Rom. 7: 23; Gal. 5: 17. (e) Matt. 26: 41; Mark 13: 33. (f) 1 Thess. 3: 13; 1 Thess. 5: 23.

Question 128: How dost thou conclude thy prayer?

Answer: "For thine is the kingdom, and the power, and the glory, forever"; that is, all these we ask of thee, because thou, being our King and almighty, art willing and able to give us all good; (a) and all this we pray for, that thereby not we, but thy holy name, may be glorified for ever. (b)

(a) Rom. 10: 11,12; 2 Pet. 2: 9. (b) John 14: 13; Jer. 33: 8,9; Ps. 115: 1.

Question 129: What does the word "Amen" signify?

Answer: "Amen" signifies, it shall truly and certainly be: for my prayer is more assuredly heard of God, than I feel in my heart that I desire these things of him. (a) (a) 2 Corinthians 1:20 For all the promises of God in him are yea, and in him Amen, unto the glory of God by us. 2 Timothy 2:13 If we believe not, yet he abideth faithful: he cannot deny himself.

(a) 2 Cor. 1: 20; 2 Tim. 2: 13.

Gracious God and Lord Jesus Christ, By Your Blessed Holy Spirit you have united us to Christ, the Vine and we are branches; grant that we would bring forth much fruit. You know our frame and remember that we are dust, and ask that you embolden us for we wrestle not against flesh and blood, but against principalities, against the powers, against the rulers of the darkness of this world, against spiritual wickedness in high places. You have called us out of the world and prayed for us because we are your own and You love your own. Yet, we constantly see another law in our members, l warring against the law of our mind and bringing us into the captivity to the law of sin which remains in us. Teach us to watch and pray that we do not enter into temptation for the spirit is willing but the flesh is week. May we ever remain vigilant and watchful so as not to fall, by your Holy Spirit. Father, we ask that You, the God of Peace sanctify us wholly, that we would be preserved blameless unto the Coming of our Savior the Lord Jesus Christ.

Thine is the Kingdom and the power and the glory forever, so that we ask, that because You are our King and almighty, that you would be willing and able to give us all good, and all this we pray for that thereby not we, but Thy Holy Name, may be glorified for ever. You know how to deliver the godly out of temptations and to reserve the unjust unto the day of judgment to be punished, and you have promised that whatever we ask, that will You do so the Father is glorified. Cleanse us from all our iniquity, pardon our sins and transgressions so that Your Church may be a praise and honor before all the nations of the earth. May all who hear of the good You do unto Your People come, and fear and tremble before You.

Not unto us, O LORD, not unto us, but unto Thy Name give glory, for Thy Mercy and for Thy truth's sake. We say a hearty and comforted "Amen" because we know our prayers are heard more assuredly of God than we often feel in our weak hearts. For all the promises of You, O God, are in Him, Christ Jesus, yea and amen unto the glory of God. Amen.

ABOUT THE AUTHOR

Nancy A. Almodovar is currently an Adjunct Professor of World Religions receiving her PhD in Philosophy and Theology at Trinity Theological Seminary. She earned her BA in Theology and MA in Philosophy and Theology with a concentration in Christian Apologetics and World Religions from Trinity as well. She is currently attending Whitefield Theological Seminary in pursuit of a Master's in Church History .

Married to Rev. Roberto Almodovar, she and her husband run a Non-Profit organization called Silent Cry Ministries. Living in Idaho, Nancy enjoys bike riding, gardening, reading and teachings others about the Free Grace of God in Justification by faith alone. She has spoken to women's groups about the Providence of God and His Care for His Creation, His Church and His children. She has also done presentations on the proofs of the Resurrection as well as apologetics.

Raised in a Christian home, after her conversion at 19, her father, Peter F. Shore Sr. began to aide her in biblical studies through the works of Reformed and Evangelical ministers such as D. Martyn Lloyd-Jones, J.C. Ryle, Martin Luther, John Calvin, John Owen and Jonathan Edwards.

A speaker, author and frequent radio guest on Calvary Perspectives and Iron Sharpens Iron, Nancy's passion is that believers will study the great doctrines of the bible in order to be better equipped to raise their children for Jesus Christ. She currently runs a Facebook group called "Old Paths for Today's Women" a group teaching women about the Doctrines of Grace which the Reformers recovered.

CPSIA information can be obtained
at www.ICGtesting.com
Printed in the USA
LVHW082142241019
635297LV00024B/264/P